MICHAEL YOUSSEF

THE

AGGRESSIVE SECULARISM, RADICAL ISLAM,

HIDDEN

AND THE FIGHT FOR OUR FUTURE

ENEMY

TYNDALE
MOMENTUM®

The nonfiction imprint of
Tyndale House Publishers, Inc.

Visit Tyndale online at www.tyndale.com.

Visit Tyndale Momentum online at www.tyndalemomentum.com.

Visit Michael Youssef at www.ltw.org.

TYNDALE, Tyndale Momentum, and Tyndale's quill logo are registered trademarks of Tyndale House Publishers, Inc. The Tyndale Momentum logo is a trademark of Tyndale House Publishers, Inc. Tyndale Momentum is the nonfiction imprint of Tyndale House Publishers, Inc., Carol Stream, Illinois.

The Hidden Enemy: Aggressive Secularism, Radical Islam, and the Fight for Our Future

Published in association with Don Gates, The Gates Group, www.gatesliterary.com.

For information about special discounts for bulk purchases, please contact Tyndale House Publishers at csresponse@tyndale.com, or call 1-800-323-9400.

Library of Congress Cataloging-in-Publication Data

Names: Youssef, Michael, author.
Title: The hidden enemy : aggressive secularism, radical Islam, and the fight for our future / Michael Youssef.
Description: Carol Stream, Illinois : Tyndale House Publishers, Inc., 2018. | Includes bibliographical references.
Identifiers: LCCN 2017049076| ISBN 9781496431455 (hc) | ISBN 9781496431462 (sc)
Subjects: LCSH: Christianity—United States. | Christianity and other religions—Islam. | Islam—Relations—Christianity. | Secularism.
Classification: LCC BR526 .Y69 2018 | DDC 211/.6—dc23 LC record available at https://lccn .loc.gov/2017049076

Printed in the United States of America

24   23   22   21   20   19   18
7   6   5   4   3   2   1

In memory of Marvin and Nadene Steinert of Bakersfield, California, with thanksgiving for our great friendship and partnership in ministry, which began in 1977.

CONTENTS

FOREWORD

THERE'S NO OTHER WAY TO PUT IT, REALLY. The moral fabric of America has been fraying for a long time—since the sixties at least. But can anyone doubt that this process has accelerated recently, that it is no longer fraying but actually tearing apart? Can we doubt that the bitter seeds that have been sown over the decades are finally coming to their ugly fruition?

Even the most fundamental things that once held us together as a culture and as a nation—free speech, for example—are struggling for life. College campuses, which were the bastion of inquiry and important centers of civil debate, have become hotbeds of fascist intolerance, so much so that speakers are being thrown off campuses simply for holding views that student mobs consider unacceptable. The Internet has become a particularly depressing maelstrom of nastiness, where actual conversation seems absolutely impossible. And of course and alas, our streets have become filled with violence. We might even bitterly conclude that the only free speech we are willing to recognize at this point is vandalism.

But let's not go that far quite yet. This book and its author give me hope. My friend Michael Youssef has been a champion of the American political experiment for a long time, so now more than ever, it is important that we heed his voice on this subject. He and I are both passionate about the foundational documents and the founding fathers, and we share a desire to make others passionate about them too.

In this, his latest book, Dr. Youssef doesn't offer a simplistic explanation of what's happening in our day. He was born in Egypt and well knows what it is like to live under a regime that doesn't value liberty or free speech. As you will come to understand, Dr. Youssef sees two enemies of America that are wittingly and unwittingly tearing apart our republic. Namely, he identifies a new type of aggressive secularism that is opening the door for radical Islam. Both are hidden in plain sight, and both are intent on destroying American freedoms.

If you're asking yourself, as I did, what aggressive secularism and radical Islam have in common, then you need to read *The Hidden Enemy*. It's eye-opening and it's vital. If we all understand what they have in common, as Dr. Youssef explains in this book, we can together begin being a part of the solution. I hope you'll join me.

Eric Metaxas
October 2017
New York City

OUR CIVILIZATION is under assault from without—and from within.

We face an *external* threat from radical, political Islam. The enemy without wants to sweep away Western civilization and impose a global caliphate.

We face an *internal* threat from a coalition of secular humanists, atheists, and leftists. The enemy within wants to erase the Judeo-Christian values our Western culture was founded on, replacing them with false dogmas of secularism, sexual liberation, hedonism, and moral relativism.

The enemy without and the enemy within have almost nothing in common. Radical, political Islam seeks to impose a theocracy that, according to strict Islamic law, calls for the oppression of women and the execution of homosexuals. The secular left is fanatical about church-state separation, feminism, and gay and transgender rights.

The enemy without and the enemy within could not be more opposed to each other. You'd think they'd constantly be at each other's throats. Yet the secular left defends and supports Islamism, and the two groups join forces to attack our Christian faith, Judeo-Christian values, Western culture, and the nation of Israel.

Often, the alliance between these groups goes largely unnoticed. Not long ago, however, representatives from the two groups publicly marched in solidarity. Like many leftist protest events, the Women's March on January 21, 2017, demanded reproductive rights (unrestricted abortions), LGBTQ rights, and wide-open borders—the usual progressive agenda. The march featured the standard collection of leftist sponsors: Planned Parenthood, the AFL–CIO, the National Center for Lesbian Rights, MoveOn.org, and more.

Oddly, however, the march organizers chose as co-chair an Islamist, Linda Sarsour, whom the *New York Times* dubbed the "Brooklyn homegirl in a hijab" in a flattering 2015 profile.[1] She's a darling of the left, whom President Obama honored as a "champion of change"—yet she advocates Sharia law in America. Her sales pitch: "You'll know when you're living under Sharia law if suddenly all your loans and credit cards become interest-free. Sounds nice, doesn't it?"[2] Sarsour neglects to mention that Sharia is incompatible with democracy, human rights, freedom of speech, freedom of religion, equality for women, LGBTQ rights, and other causes liberals claim to support.

The progressive left's fawning adoration of Ms. Sarsour is a vivid demonstration of the strange alliance between these two ideologically opposed groups. But this is far from an isolated phenomenon, as you'll see in these pages. The secular left and fanatical Islam have made a devil's bargain. Their mutual goal: the overthrow of Western culture and Judeo-Christian values.

How do we confront these enemies—the enemy within and the enemy without? Should we form a political action committee;

hire a lobbying firm in Washington, DC; hold a protest march and flex our political muscle? Should we try to beat the Islamists and the secular left at their own game?

No. As God's Word tells us, there is only one way to win: We must "be strong in the Lord and in his mighty power" (Ephesians 6:10, NLT). We must never forget that Jesus taught us to love our adversaries, pray for them, and do good to them (Luke 6:27-28). The battle against Islamic and secular extremism is not one we can win with weapons of hate. The battle for truth can be won only by the power of Christlike love. Without His love, we're just clanging gongs and cymbals—making a lot of noise while accomplishing nothing (1 Corinthians 13:1).

But the enemy without and the enemy within are only *two of the three deadly threats* to the future of our children and grandchildren. There's also *the hidden enemy*.

In fact, the greatest threat we face comes from this third adversary, one that hides from view. We don't want to admit that this threat exists, because then we'll have to deal with it. We'll have to struggle with it every day—vigilantly and prayerfully.

Later in the book, the identity of this hidden enemy will become clear. First, though, I want to help you understand the grave threat we face from our two very visible ideological opponents. Turn the page with me. Let me show you how to achieve a true and lasting victory over the enemy without, the enemy within, and ultimately—yes—the hidden enemy.

THE TRUTH ABOUT OUR FUTURE

I WAS BORN INTO the Coptic Christian community in Egypt during a time of great social change.

In 1952, just four years after my birth, a group of nationalist military leaders launched a coup d'état, forcing Egypt's king Farouk to flee into exile. The revolutionary government abolished the monarchy, established a republic, and soon ended the British occupation of Egypt (which had begun in 1882). The leaders of the revolution brought both Islamic and socialist dogma into the new Egyptian government—the first time in history, to my knowledge, that you find socialism married to Islam.

Colonel Gamal Abdel Nasser proclaimed himself chairman of the Revolutionary Command Council and prime minister of the Republic in February 1954. Two years later, he was elected president. He became, in effect, the dictator of an Islamist-socialist military regime. Islamism and socialism are both totalitarian political systems that recognize no limits to the authority of the state. Both seek to control every aspect of public and private life.

So it should have come as no surprise when Nasser filled leadership positions in the government, corporations, and banks with army generals. By 1956, he began nationalizing all foreign commercial holdings, beginning with the Anglo-French-owned Suez Canal. He then nationalized foreign banks, including Barclays Bank, where two of my older brothers worked. He also nationalized private Egyptian companies and land holdings, placing large landowners under house arrest.

The small oil distributorship where my father worked was soon taken over by the state. I vividly recall the day my father came home from work, sat us down, and explained that he was out of a job. He had arrived at the office to find army officers standing guard. They told him the company was now the property of the state, and they sent my father and his associates home.

Another consequence of the Islamic-socialist takeover: The lives of Coptic Christians became much more difficult. The Copts' fortunes had risen and fallen over the centuries, but by the early 1900s, Christians and Muslims had been treated equally. Though Islam had been Egypt's dominant religion for more than a millennium, Christianity's roots in Egypt were much deeper. In fact, the Christian faith had thrived in Egypt from the first century on. According to Acts 2:10, Egyptian Jews were at the first Pentecost in Jerusalem, where they witnessed the coming of the Holy Spirit and heard Peter preach. After deciding to follow Christ, they returned to Alexandria and began spreading their new faith. Mark the Evangelist (the writer of the Gospel of Mark) arrived there around AD 49 and became the first bishop of Alexandria. By the second century, Christianity was the majority religion in Egypt, and Alexandria became the leading center of Christian theology for more than two hundred years.

Fast forward to the mid-600s, when Muslim hordes invaded Egypt from Arabia. After gaining control, those early Islamists offered the Christian majority population three alternatives: convert to Islam, die by the sword, or pay the *jizya* tax and accept their status as *dhimmi* (non-Muslim citizens of the Islamic state). Wealthy Egyptians could afford to pay the 15 to 25 percent jizya tax. But most of the Coptic Christians were too poor to pay. Not wanting to die by the sword, many pretended to convert to Islam. They outwardly practiced the Muslim religion while inwardly trying to maintain their Christian faith. Believing one thing while practicing another proved too difficult for many of these conquered Christians. The harsh Islamic religion scorched the gospel out of their hearts, like the seeds that fell on stony ground in the Lord's parable of the sower. That's why a majority of Egyptians are Muslims today.

Despite their long presence in Egypt, Christians became second-class citizens after the revolution. They could no longer be heads of banks, corporations, universities, or local governments. Highly educated Christians were relegated to minimum-wage jobs, and less-qualified Muslims were favored for career advancement.

The Nasser regime encouraged an atmosphere of hostility toward Christians. Muslims began harassing Christians without cause. When I was at school or just walking down the street, I was often mocked, insulted, and sometimes beaten by young Muslims who knew I came from a Christian family.

Not all Muslims were hostile to me. I had some very good friends at school who came from moderate, enlightened Muslim homes. (Note: Even now, most Muslims do not fall into the extreme Islamist camp, but these voices of reason are largely muted in our world today.) It was primarily the working-class and illiterate Muslims who made life difficult for me and other Christians. Some parts of town were militant Muslim strongholds, and I didn't dare enter those neighborhoods alone, especially at night.

President Nasser clamped down on churches and Christian organizations. He revived old Ottoman-era laws restricting the rights of the dhimmi (Christians and Jews). For example, no new church could be built without the permission of the head of state. Also, no evangelism or missionary work was permitted outside church walls. These laws are still enforced today.

Nasser increased the number of paid and unpaid informants to the point that you never knew who might be a government spy. In businesses, in schools, and on the street, everyone was afraid to say anything critical of the government. Even at home, people spoke only in whispers, fearing an informant might overhear. The government employed student informants to report on their classmates. My parents warned me to be extremely careful about anything I said at school.

As a young man, I went to libraries and checked out books on American freedom and American ideals. I was fascinated, even mesmerized, by the freedoms Americans enjoyed. I was especially drawn to ideas such as freedom of speech and freedom of religion. At the same time, I worried that someone at the library might report to the government the kinds of books I was checking out. Yet I couldn't stop reading and dreaming of America.

WHY I CHERISH FREEDOM

In 1977, I realized my dream and moved to the United States; in 1984, I achieved my goal of becoming a citizen. My early years living under a socialist dictatorship, immersed in a hostile Muslim culture, gave me a perspective on our American freedoms that many native-born Americans don't have. In my heart, I was an American long before I became a citizen. I had yearned to be an American years before I ever reached these shores.

After arriving here, I was dismayed to see how many Americans had so little regard for their own history and the blessings of freedom they enjoyed. People who had lived in America all their lives didn't understand what a privilege it was to live here and to be free to speak their minds, to vote, and to openly share their faith. Too many Americans took freedom for granted. Having grown up under Islamo-socialist totalitarianism, that's something I'll never do.

Why do so many people around the world dream of coming to America? Why don't people dream of finding a better life in Venezuela? Or Iran? Or North Korea? Or Saudi Arabia? Because there is no freedom in those countries, nor economic opportunity, the great by-product of freedom. America attracts immigrants because America offers liberty.

One foundational American freedom is the ability to speak the truth without fear of punishment or arrest. At one time, that freedom was a fact of American life, as fixed and unassailable as Mount Rushmore. Today, that freedom is under assault as never before. There is a real possibility we may lose that freedom altogether. Some examples:

Example 1: Former Georgetown University law professor and gay rights activist Chai Feldblum helped draft federal legislation on sexual orientation. She is guided by the notion that whenever gay rights come in conflict with First Amendment religious liberty, the First Amendment must give way. She once told an interviewer,

"I'm having a hard time coming up with any case in which religious liberty should win."[1]

Example 2: After the deadly December 2, 2015, mass shooting by two Islamists at the Inland Regional Center in San Bernardino, California (fourteen dead, twenty-two wounded), many Christians offered their thoughts and prayers on social media. The secular left responded with a scathing backlash.

Arthur Delaney and Sam Stein, writing for the *Huffington Post,* said, "Every time multiple people have been gunned down in a mass shooting, all these officials can seemingly do is rush to offer their useless thoughts and prayers."[2] *Washington Post* columnist Gene Weingarten tweeted, "Dear 'thoughts and prayers' people: Please shut up and slink away. You are the problem, and everyone knows it."[3] *Daily Kos* founder Markos Moulitsas tweeted, "How many dead people did those thoughts and prayers bring back to the life?" Journalist Andrew Husband went even further, posting an ugly, obscene comment directed at those who pray after a tragedy.[4] Clearly, we have turned a corner in our culture if offers of prayer are met with howls of derision and hostility.

Example 3: During the 2016 Democratic National Convention in Philadelphia, the gay activist group Equality Forum held an event to celebrate the Supreme Court decision imposing recognition of same-sex marriage on all fifty states. The organizers also discussed future plans for advancing the gay agenda. One participant, Gautam Raghavan of the Gill Foundation, made it clear that they believe "gay rights" should always supersede the First Amendment: "I want to be careful that we don't say there is a kind of balance between equality [i.e., gay rights] and religious freedom."[5]

Other issues discussed at the event included plans to impose transgender bathroom laws nationwide, promote gay sex education in public schools, and withdraw Title IX funding from religious schools that oppose the gay agenda. So expect the gay-rights assault on First Amendment freedom to intensify.[6]

Example 4: Professor Mark Tushnet teaches constitutional law at Harvard Law School. A few months after the death of conservative Supreme Court justice Antonin Scalia, Tushnet wrote a blog post declaring victory over conservatives: "The culture wars are over; they lost, we won. . . . For liberals, the question now is how to deal with the losers in the culture wars. That's mostly a question of tactics. My own judgment is that taking a hard line ('You lost, live with it') is better than trying to accommodate the losers. . . . (And taking a hard line seemed to work reasonably well in Germany and Japan after 1945.)"[7]

I could list many more examples—of Christian bakers, florists, and photographers being forced by the government to violate their conscience and provide services to same-sex weddings; of Christian businesses being forced to pay for abortion-inducing drugs for their employees; of Christian parents being told by school districts that they have no right to homeschool their children (most recently in the San Benito High School District in California in 2016).

The First Amendment guarantees our right to speak God's truth—but our First Amendment freedoms are under a sustained and determined assault by the secular left. We live in a world that rejects the very notion of verifiable truth. The pundits and social critics of our age have, in fact, declared the death of objective truth. Following the 2016 election, *Washington Post* columnist Amy B. Wang observed,

It's official: Truth is dead. Facts are passé. . . .

Oxford Dictionaries has selected "post-truth" as 2016's international word of the year, after the contentious "Brexit" referendum and an equally divisive U.S. presidential election caused usage of the adjective to skyrocket, according to the Oxford University Press.

The dictionary defines "post-truth" as "relating to or denoting circumstances in which objective facts are less influential in shaping public opinion than appeals to emotion and personal belief."[8]

Truth no longer matters to many of the people around us. Secularists elevate subjective opinion over objective truth. Facts have been replaced by emotions. Those who stand firm for God's truth are widely mocked and condemned. Yet God still calls you and me to take a stand for His truth in a world that despises truth.

Journalists used to try, at least, to present the news fairly and objectively. Old-school journalist Ted Koppel, who hosted ABC's *Nightline* for twenty-five years, decried the loss of factual, unbiased reporting in an op-ed he wrote for the *Washington Post* in 2010. He lamented the death of "a long-gone era of television journalism, when the networks considered the collection and dissemination of substantive and unbiased news to be a public trust." He criticized MSNBC anchor-commentator Keith Olbermann, who "draws more than 1 million like-minded viewers to his program every night precisely because he is avowedly, unabashedly and monotonously partisan. . . . While I can appreciate the financial logic of drowning television viewers in a flood of opinions designed to confirm [networks'] own biases, the trend is not good for the republic."[9]

Olbermann fired back the next day, blaming journalists like Koppel for "worshiping before the false god of utter objectivity. . . . The kind of television journalism he eulogizes, failed this country because when truth was needed, all we got were facts—most of which were lies anyway. The journalism failed, and those who practiced it failed, and Mr. Koppel failed."[10]

Koppel stood his ground, defining objective reporting as giving people "enough information that you can make intelligent decisions of your own."[11] He went on to warn that intensely partisan cable news shows and talk radio programs were dividing America into hostile partisan camps.

Yet even Ted Koppel could not have foreseen how bitterly divided America would be today. A deep ideological rift separates the American people because both sides are being fed a steady diet of venomous emotions, rage and hate, character assassination, extreme opinions, advocacy journalism, and violent images—all mislabeled as "news." Many reporters don't care about the truth any more, and neither do most news consumers. We just want programs that confirm our biases.

Likewise, many of our public universities are no longer devoted to objective truth and learning. Many have become factories for brainwashing students in "politically correct" ideas. Students are not trained to be wise and well-informed but are simply indoctrinated into the party line. They graduate knowing little about the classics, the humanities, economics, or history. But they know who their political and ideological enemies are.

The erosion of a respect for truth has been going on for decades. In 1987, activist Jesse Jackson—who was running for the Democratic presidential nomination—joined student protesters at Stanford University as they chanted, "Hey, hey, ho, ho, Western

Civ has got to go!" And the Stanford administration yielded to the demands of the activists, dropping the Western Civilization requirement from their catalog. Homer, Plato, Augustine, and Thomas Aquinas disappeared from the list of required texts. Students at one of the greatest universities in the world were cut off from their history, their culture, and their heritage of great thinking and truth.[12]

In recent years, the attack on truth in general—and biblical truth in particular—has accelerated. Most heartbreaking of all, some so-called "evangelical" leaders are tossing biblical truth overboard, stripping Scripture of its authority and replacing objective truth with so-called "narrative." Certain leaders no longer view the Bible as God's inspired and authoritative Word but as a collection of comforting and instructive stories.

One formerly evangelical leader complains that orthodox, conservative Christianity has "shown a pervasive disdain for other religions of the world," whose members we should view "not as enemies but as beloved neighbors, and whenever possible, as dialogue partners and even collaborators."[13]

Although Jesus was a master at listening and asking questions to get to people's real needs, He never compromised the truth. He never said, "Collaborating with other religions will set you free." He said, "If you hold to my teaching, you are really my disciples. *Then you will know the truth, and the truth will set you free*" (John 8:31-32, emphasis mine). Truth comes from the words of Jesus, and only His truth will set us free.

Yes, we should love Muslims, Hindus, Buddhists, atheists, and people of all religions and worldviews. We must reach out to them with the good news of Jesus Christ, empathizing with them and listening to their concerns and needs. But we can never become partners or collaborators with falsehood.

In a post-truth world, embracing all belief systems as equal may sound like an open-minded, openhearted idea. But Jesus was intolerant of falsehood. That's why He declared, "I am the way and the truth and the life. No one comes to the Father *except through me*" (John 14:6, emphasis mine).

I should note, by the way, that the same author who says Christians should "collaborate" with other religions also wrote that Jesus, in John 14:6, didn't really mean what He seems to say. The Lord's claim that "no one comes to the Father except through me" doesn't really mean that Jesus is the only way to God and heaven, according to this author. In other words, two thousand years of biblical scholarship have been wrong, and John 14:6 has been waiting all these centuries for this author to arrive on the scene and tell us what Jesus *really* meant.

The author mischaracterizes the evangelical interpretation of John 14:6, describing it as a way to "exclude the outsiders" by using "mental markers or belief markers" about Jesus and suggests that evangelicals believe that "God will reject everyone except people who share [our] doctrinal viewpoints" about Jesus.[14] That's a straw-man argument because that is *not* what evangelicals believe. John 14:6 does not call people to mentally accept a "doctrinal viewpoint" about Jesus. In that verse, *Jesus calls us to a relationship with Himself.* That is how John 14:6 has been understood since the first century AD, and that verse needs no radical reinterpretation for the twenty-first century.

When I see speakers and authors working so hard to force God's Word to say what it clearly does *not* say, I hear the apostle Paul whispering in my ear, "The Spirit clearly says that in later times some will abandon the faith and follow deceiving spirits" (1 Timothy 4:1). In Jesus' high priestly prayer before going to the cross, he prayed, "Sanctify them by the truth; your word is truth" (John 17:17). All too often, however, we have polluted God's truth with borrowings from the false religions and philosophies of our culture. No one is sanctified by adulterated "truth."

If we as individuals reject or distort God's truth, we rob the truth of its power to set us free. The result: We become morally and spiritually enslaved. And when an entire culture rejects God's truth? That culture opens itself up to bondage. We are already seeing this process of cultural enslavement taking place in post-Christian Western nations like Great Britain, France, Germany, Belgium, and the Scandinavian countries. In some communities Islamic Sharia law is moving into the void left by the collapse of biblical Christianity.

In Great Britain, for example, an Islamic firebrand named Abu Izzadeen has been leading a campaign to impose Sharia law across the nation. Following his release from prison for funding terrorism in 2011, Izzadeen proclaimed himself "director for Waltham Forest Muslims" (Waltham Forest is a major borough in East London) and began organizing support for his campaign to impose Sharia on the entire borough. His organization's yellow leaflets have been posted to lampposts and shop windows, proclaiming, "You are entering a Sharia-controlled zone. Islamic rules enforced. No alcohol. No gambling. No music or concerts. No porn or prostitution. No drugs or smoking. Sharia—a better society."[15]

I won't argue that we'd be worse off in a society without gambling, porn, prostitution, and drugs. But a society without music? A society without freedom? A society ruled by fear? A society in which women have no rights and are treated as chattel slaves?

A society in which "Islamic rules" are enforced with medieval brutality by Sharia tribunals? And there are already about eighty-five Sharia councils dispensing Quranic "justice" across Great Britain.[16]

American Islamist groups are currently trying to establish Sharia courts in the United States. Many misguided Americans, primarily from the post-truth left, support Islamism and the importation of Sharia to America, despite Sharia's legacy of punishing lawbreakers by flogging, amputation, and stoning. Please understand: *Islamist* is not a synonym for *Islamic*. Islamism is radical, activist, political Islam, the movement that seeks to impose Islamic principles and Sharia law on public and political life. Many on the left think that conservative objections to importing Sharia courts into America are paranoid—"Those mean conservatives just want to squash the rights of the poor, marginalized Muslims."

Why do liberals and progressives support Islamists—the most anti-progressive culture on the planet, a culture that oppresses women and executes homosexuals? How do we explain the irrational behavior of the post-truth left?

I think it comes down to a concept called *underdogma*, a term coined by columnist Michael Prell. Underdogma is a way of perceiving reality that divides the world into two camps—the strong and the weak, the powerful and the powerless, the overdog and the underdog. Underdogma, says Prell, is the "reflexive opposition to the more powerful overdog, and automatic support for the less powerful underdog."[17]

In his book *Underdogma*, Prell cites two statements by then-Senator Barack Obama during Supreme Court confirmation proceedings. When John Roberts was nominated as the US Supreme

Court's chief justice, Senator Obama expressed his view that "the role of justice is to favor the 'weak' over the 'strong.'" And Senator Obama complained that nominee Samuel Alito "consistently sides on behalf of the powerful against the powerless."[18] To Senator Obama, the role of the judicial system is not to dispense justice impartially according to the law and the Constitution, but to show favoritism to the underdog. This bias toward the underdog is pervasive throughout the post-truth left.

People who view the world through a lens of underdogma do not arrive at their views on the basis of logic and facts. They are led by emotion. A 2007 study, published in the scientific journal *Personality and Social Psychology Bulletin*, showed how underdogma sways people's thinking.

Professor Joseph Vandello of the University of South Florida asked test subjects to read a one-page essay about the Israeli-Palestinian conflict from the perspective of each side. Test subjects were divided into two groups. Group A was shown a map depicting Israel as geographically large with Palestinian land as small. Group B was shown a map in which little Israel was surrounded by larger Egypt, Jordan, Syria, and so forth. The two groups were asked to identify the underdog in the conflict.

Seventy percent of Group A identified the Palestinians as the underdogs, and 53 percent said they sided with the Palestinians. Sixty-two percent of Group B identified the Israelis as the underdogs, and almost 77 percent sided with Israel. Both groups were provided with identical facts, but different maps—and the maps influenced their sympathies.[19]

It's not enough to ask, "Who is the underdog in this conflict?" We need to ask who is right and who is wrong, who is just and who is unjust. When deciding whether to support Israel or the

Palestinians, we should ask ourselves two questions: 1. If Israel's enemies dropped their weapons today, what would happen? (Answer: Peace would break out.) 2. If Israel dropped its weapons today, what would happen? (Answer: War would break out.)

The Palestinians are weak and poor—but that doesn't make the annihilation of Israel a just cause. We need to base our views on principles of truth and justice—not on underdogma. Similarly, we need to make decisions about whether to import Sharia courts into America based on truth and justice—not underdogma. If we do not take a stand for God's truth in our post-truth culture, we will find ourselves enslaved in our own land.

The Israelites, long before the Babylonian Exile, practiced the same approach to truth that many practice today. They didn't believe God's ways were sufficient any longer. They wanted to import the "truth" of the Canaanites, Amorites, Philistines, Assyrians, and other pagan cultures. Israel paid a heavy price—military defeat, the destruction of their nation, and the exile of their people—for ignoring God's warnings against mingling pagan practices with their laws and worship.

God continues to warn us not to tamper with the truth of His gospel. Decades ago, the late Dr. Francis A. Schaeffer predicted that the evangelical church would be seduced into spiritual adultery, and that all of Western civilization would pay the price:

> A large segment of the evangelical world has become seduced by the world spirit of this present age. And more than this, we can expect the future to be a further disaster if the evangelical world does not take a stand for biblical truth and morality in the full spectrum of life. *For the evangelical accommodation to the world of our age represents*

the removal of the last barrier against the breakdown of our culture. And with the final removal of this barrier will come social chaos and the rise of authoritarianism in some form to restore social order.[20]

Because of our failure to stand for God's truth, Schaeffer warned, the world would sink into chaos, the people would panic—and they would surrender their liberties to an authoritarian government.

I believe the events Dr. Schaeffer envisioned are already taking shape. America is fracturing into warring camps of left versus right, of haves versus have-nots, of blacks versus browns versus whites. There is a growing backlash against income inequality—the concentration of more and more wealth in fewer and fewer hands. In American cities, peaceful protest marches are turning into bloody riots—and police are often standing back and abandoning neighborhoods to the mobs.

America is $20 trillion in debt and running annual deficits of about half a trillion dollars. Just the interest on the national debt is approaching the amount we spend every year on national defense—which could leave us unable to defend ourselves against foreign enemies. What do you think will happen to our society if the government can no longer issue checks for Social Security, welfare benefits, medical benefits, and the federal payroll?

For several years, Pentagon planners have been partnering with social scientists in academia to study matters of US security, including the possibility of the collapse of American society and large-scale civil disorder within our borders. The Pentagon's multimillion dollar Minerva Research Initiative has quietly been working with universities around the country, seeking to understand how to contain the "social contagion" of mass panic and restore order in the midst of social upheaval and collapse.[21]

In 2016, two independent researchers—Matthew MacWilliams of the University of Massachusetts Amherst and Marc Hetherington of Vanderbilt University in Tennessee—determined that there was a growing desire for authoritarianism in the American electorate. According to journalist Amanda Taub, the researchers found that frightened voters, worried about social disintegration in America, were looking "for strong leaders who promise to take whatever action necessary to protect them."[22]

I hate the thought of America being reduced to such a state. When I lived under a dictatorship in Egypt, I saw how everyone, from journalists to pastors to students, had to obey the whims of the dictator—or face the consequences. The land of my birth was a police state where your neighbors might turn you in to the authorities if you voiced a minor criticism of the government or Islam. I thought I had left such oppressive practices behind when I emigrated to America. But in recent years, I've seen stirrings of the same authoritarianism in America that I once feared in Egypt.

Is it too late for Western civilization to rediscover the great truths on which it was founded? Is it too late for the church to regain its voice and return to its biblical roots?

No—not quite, not yet.

But we must be aware of the forces arrayed against us. Islamic extremism is coming at us from one direction, seeking to destroy the Christian faith and Western values. Secular fundamentalism is coming at us from the opposite direction, with the same goal of destruction. These are the enemies without and the enemies within. Collision is imminent. If we are to survive, we need to do more than simply brace for impact.

In the pages that follow, I will present a clear and practical action agenda for renewal and revival, rooted in the eternal truth of God's Word. You and I *can*—and *must*—become warriors for God's truth in a culture that is increasingly hostile to the truth. We must rediscover what it means to be the people of God's truth in a post-truth world.

2

THE TRUTH BE HANGED

HEATHER MAC DONALD is a respected scholar, author, and social commentator, a graduate of Yale University and Stanford Law School. She has written for the *Wall Street Journal*, the *Washington Post*, and the *New York Times*. In 2016, she wrote a book called *The War on Cops: How the New Attack on Law and Order Makes Everyone Less Safe*. The book includes a critique of Black Lives Matter and other radical groups that empower themselves by claiming to be victims of a racist police culture.

On Thursday, April 6, 2017, Heather Mac Donald was scheduled to give a talk to a student audience at Claremont McKenna College in Southern California. She was in the Athenaeum, a campus auditorium, when a group of about 250 protesters surrounded the building and blocked all the entrances, forcibly preventing any students, faculty, or guests from entering the hall to hear her speak. The radicals shouted "Black lives matter!" and directed expletives at police. They also yelled accusations that Ms. Mac Donald was a "white supremacist fascist." They shoved and threatened student journalists trying to cover the incident for the student newspaper.[1]

It's worth noting, by the way, that one of the latest tactics of the left involves smearing anyone who disagrees with them as a "white supremacist" or some other offensive label. Their goal is to turn their political opponents into outcasts or pariahs. If they label you a white supremacist, they make you radioactive and untouchable. Your friends will hesitate to associate with you or defend you because they might be the next ones smeared. Deliberately destroying another person's reputation is one of the most evil things one human being can do to another, which is why "You shall not give false testimony against your neighbor" is the ninth commandment.

When the activists blocked the entrances, shut down the event, and threatened student journalists, the nervous college officials decided not to intervene. Citing safety concerns, they allowed the protesters to control the situation. Ms. Mac Donald gave her talk to a mostly empty auditorium as the thugs banged on the auditorium windows. Her talk (which was cut short by campus police) was live streamed on the college website and later uploaded to YouTube.

After the talk, Ms. Mac Donald was hustled out a rear exit by police. The radicals, who claimed to represent a group that called itself "students of color at the Claremont Colleges," were permitted to deny the speaker and the audience their First Amendment rights.

A lengthy college investigation included the review of "available video and photographic evidence" and witness interviews. Of the estimated 250 protesters (most of whom were not students at the college), twelve Claremont McKenna students were named "potential participants in the blockade." Several months later, ten students were charged with violations of college policy. Five were suspended for six months to a year, two were placed on probation, and three were cleared.[2]

The day after the incident at Claremont McKenna, David W. Oxtoby, the president of another Claremont institution, Pomona College, sent out an e-mail declaring that his campus is committed to "the exercise of free speech and academic freedom . . . while affirming the value of nondiscrimination and condemning racism in all forms."[3] A few days later, a radical student group at Pomona College answered the president's message with a series of strident demands, including an apology from Oxtoby for his e-mail, punishment of the student-run newspaper that reported on the Claremont McKenna incident, and the banning of conservative speakers like Ms. Mac Donald from campus. (In their letter, the radical group labeled Ms. Mac Donald "a fascist, a white supremacist, a warhawk, a transphobe, a queerphobe, a classist, and ignorant of interlocking systems of domination that produce the lethal conditions under which oppressed peoples are forced to live.")[4]

Heather Mac Donald doesn't fit any of those labels, but the truth doesn't seem to matter to these extremists. They reject any notion of objective truth, concluding their demands with this chilling statement:

> Historically, white supremacy has venerated the idea of objectivity, and wielded a dichotomy of "subjectivity vs. objectivity" as a means of silencing oppressed peoples. The idea that there is a single truth—"the Truth"—is a construct of the Euro-West that is deeply rooted in the Enlightenment, which was a movement that also

described Black and Brown people as both subhuman and impervious to pain. This construction is a myth and white supremacy, imperialism, colonization, capitalism, and the United States of America are all of its progeny. The idea that the truth is an entity for which we must search, in matters that endanger our abilities to exist in open spaces, is an attempt to silence oppressed peoples. . . . The idea that we must subject ourselves routinely to the hate speech of fascists who want for us not to exist plays on the same Eurocentric constructs that believed Black people to be impervious to pain and apathetic to the brutal and violent conditions of white supremacy.[5]

This paragraph is loaded with so much Marxist-Maoist jargon that it may be difficult for you to make any sense of it. So here is my paraphrase of that statement: "We reject the notion of truth. The idea of 'objective truth' was invented by white racists as a means of oppressing people of color. The very notion of truth endangers our lives. 'Free speech' is a tool of white racists for spouting hate. We have a right to intimidate and silence those who disagree with us."

There have been other instances of radical student groups making extreme demands at Claremont schools. Journalist Charlotte Allen concludes, "It's hard to know why all of this is taking place at once at all five Claremont colleges: the domino effect; social-justice chic; too many classes in colonialism, oppression, and white male hegemony? But it's odd that the dominant activity on some of America's most expensive and elite campuses, supposedly devoted to the honing of the intellect, seems to be bullying and intimidating other people."[6]

The death of freedom always begins with the abolition of truth. These young radicals demand their own right to free speech even as they trample on the First Amendment rights of others. The bullying tactics and anti-truth proclamations of these young people at Claremont McKenna are nothing new. This is the same bombastic, deceitful jargon that followers of Marx, Lenin, Mao, Ho Chi Minh, and Pol Pot often spew. They reject truth and objectivity. They make demands. They intimidate and bully opponents. David Horowitz puts it this way: "Inside every progressive is a totalitarian screaming to get out."

And when campus administrators and police officials surrender to the thuggery and demands of these radicals—hoping to appease them by backing down—the protesters are only emboldened. They come back with even more unreasonable demands and greater violence. This is how a tiny minority of committed extremists assert their will and infringe on the rights of the majority. History shows that giving way in the face of hoodlums always ends badly, usually with violence and death, and sometimes with armed revolution.

This post-truth world will lie about you and destroy you. If you speak out for traditional marriage, people will call you a bigot and a homophobe. They'll destroy your reputation, your livelihood, and your family, if they can. They will pose as loving and tolerant people, while branding *you* a hater. As Christians, we are to hate the sin while loving the sinner, just as Jesus did. He told the woman caught in adultery that he did not condemn her—but he also told her to leave her life of sin. But this post-truth culture demands that we embrace *both* the sinner *and* the sin.

We live in a post-truth world, so many people and institutions have rejected the very concept of truth and become incapable of distinguishing between truth and lies. We live in a time of moral and spiritual confusion like that described by the nineteenth-century poet James Russell Lowell in "The Present Crisis":

Once to every man and nation comes the moment to decide,
In the strife of Truth with Falsehood, for the good or evil side;
Some great cause, God's new Messiah, offering each the bloom
*   or blight,*
Parts the goats upon the left hand, and the sheep upon the right,
And the choice goes by forever 'twixt that darkness and
*   that light. . . .*

Careless seems the great Avenger; history's pages but record
One death-grapple in the darkness 'twixt old systems and
*   the Word;*
Truth forever on the scaffold, Wrong forever on the throne,—
Yet that scaffold sways the future, and, behind the dim unknown,
Standeth God within the shadow, keeping watch above his own.

Yes, Truth is on the scaffold with a noose around its neck—and the enemies of truth have megaphones, microphones, and printing presses. Their attitude is *Truth be hanged*. Wrong is on the throne of this world.

A RATIONAL WORLD, A RATIONAL FAITH, A RATIONAL GOD

When those in authority refuse to defend law-abiding citizens and instead allow rebellious thugs to run riot, chaos and social disorder are sure to follow. This is what happens when we no longer stand for the truth but give way before the self-proclaimed enemies of the truth.

Yet the American government exists to defend constitutional rights and the freedom to speak the truth without fear of violence or intimidation. That is not merely my opinion. That is a fundamental principle set forth in America's founding documents, notably in the Declaration of Independence: "We hold these truths to be self-evident, that all men are created equal, that they are endowed by their Creator with certain unalienable Rights, that among these are Life, Liberty and the pursuit of Happiness. That to secure these rights, *Governments are instituted among Men*, deriving their just powers from the consent of the governed" (emphasis added).

The apostle Paul also set forth the principle that government exists to protect its citizens and to restrain and suppress evildoers: "The authorities that exist have been established by God. Consequently, whoever rebels against the authority is rebelling against what God has instituted, and those who do so will bring judgment on themselves. For rulers hold no terror for those who do right, but for those who do wrong" (Romans 13:1-3).

Our Western civilization was founded on a belief in the central importance of rational thought, objective truth, and timeless biblical principles. For centuries, Christian thinkers—great men of the faith like the apostles, Augustine, Origen, Calvin, Luther, C. S. Lewis, John Stott, Norman Geisler, and William Lane Craig—have taught that the Christian faith is reasonable and based on evidence. The Bible does not tell us to practice "blind faith," but a faith that is rooted in objective reality. No other religion is based on the objective evidence of history—only Christianity.

Truth is a bedrock concept in the Christian faith. Paul tells us that God "wants all people to be saved and to come to a knowledge of the truth" (1 Timothy 2:4). And Jesus told a group of new followers, "If you hold to my teaching, you are really my disciples. Then you will know the truth, and the truth will set you free" (John 8:31-32). Jesus also claimed to be the very personification of truth: "I am the way and the truth and the life. No one comes to the Father except through me" (John 14:6).

The concept of truth was as essential to the Old Testament as it is in the New. God, speaking through the prophet Isaiah, said, "I have not spoken in secret, from somewhere in a land of darkness; I have not said to Jacob's descendants, 'Seek me in vain.' I, the LORD, speak the truth; I declare what is right" (Isaiah 45:19).

Many people, both Christians and non-Christians, fail to understand the important role of verified, objective truth in the Christian life. They have the mistaken notion that faith is belief without any evidence, or even belief contradicted by the evidence. Many people, both Christians and non-Christians, think that science and Christianity are irreconcilable kingdoms of thought.

The late agnostic paleontologist Stephen Jay Gould tried to resolve the conflict between people of science and people of faith by stating that religion and science are "non-overlapping magisteria."[7] A magisterium is a realm of authority or teaching. Gould was saying, in effect, that the church should stick to matters of faith and leave science to the scientists, and that scientists should stick to science and not get involved in matters of God, spirit, morality, and religion. Dr. Gould meant well, but it's simply not possible to neatly divide reality into two "non-overlapping" realms of truth, one factual, the other purely spiritual and moral.

All of reality is one. It is all created by God. There is nothing under the authority of science that is not also under the authority of God the Creator. Our world is a rational world, our faith is a rational faith, our God is a rational God, and we are to approach spiritual reality with the same inquiring, reasoning intelligence that we would bring to a science lab.

God, who created the human mind, tells us we are to use our reasoning ability, as well as our spirits and emotions, when we interact with Him (see Isaiah 1:18). And the apostle Peter tells us that when we share our faith with others, we should always be ready to back up our beliefs with sound reasoning and solid evidence (see 1 Peter 3:15). The truth of God's Word can be logically defended. The Bible is not an irrational document. From Genesis to Revelation, God's Word makes good sense.

You might ask, doesn't the Bible tell us not to lean on our own human understanding (Proverbs 3:5-6)? Doesn't the Bible tell us that the just (God's righteous followers) shall live by faith (Galatians 3:11)? Aren't we supposed to simply trust God, regardless of whether or not His Word seems to make logical sense?

The truth is that all faith comes from God, and God imparts faith to us by many means—through the still small voice of the Holy Spirit within us, through the message of God's Word, through the gracious words of fellow Christians, through the experiences of our daily lives, and, yes, through evidence and reason. God has many ways to draw us to His truth and many ways to persuade us that we can rely on His truth.

So we have faith—a faith that is founded on, and grounded in, reason and truth. The ultimate enemy of all truth—especially God's truth—is Satan. Jesus describes our adversary this way: "He was a murderer from the beginning, not holding to the truth, for there is no truth in him. When he lies, he speaks his native language, for he is a liar and the father of lies" (John 8:44).

THE BEGINNING OF THE END

I believe Western civilization was born in 1517, when Martin Luther ignited the fires of the Protestant Reformation. Of course, Western civilization—the accumulated traditions, social norms, belief systems, and political structures associated with the West—is truly made up of many strands of history and culture. These include the classical Greek and Roman cultures, the Jewish traditions, and the Middle Eastern Christian religion. All of these strands of culture demonstrate a deep respect for truth.

But in October 1517, when Martin Luther nailed his Ninety-Five Theses on the door of All Saints' Church in Wittenberg, Germany, he brought all of these strands of history and culture together in one towering document. He was declaring that truth is found not in any governmental or church authority, but in Scripture. In Theses 1 through 40, Luther criticized the Roman Catholic Church for teaching people to rely on the corrupt church practice of selling indulgences rather than teaching them the gospel of repentance and forgiveness of sin laid out in the Scriptures. Luther was teaching the importance of objective truth, human freedom, and equality before God.

In Theses 41 through 52, Luther accused the church of building its edifices from the "skin, flesh, and bones" of God's people. This is an early assertion of human rights—the right of the people to be taught the truth of God and not be exploited for ungodly profit. In Theses 53 through 66, Luther returned to the theme of truth, stating that the treasure of God's church is not silver and gold, but the truth of the gospel. In Theses 67 through 91, Luther made several devastating rational arguments against the selling of indulgences. If the pope had the authority to take away guilt for sins, Luther asked, why did he do so only for money?

In Theses 92 through 95, Luther exhorted all believers to imitate Christ, to exemplify a life of repentance, and to avoid placing any reliance upon the false security of indulgences. In short, Luther argued that the behavior of the church should be determined by the truth of Scripture, not by the corrupt will of man. Because there is no biblical basis for the practice of selling the forgiveness of God for cash donations, such practices have no foundation in God's truth. Anything that does not align with the truth of God's Word is falsehood.

Luther taught the church and European culture to respect truth and anchor it to Scripture. Western societies have operated on a foundation of reason and objective truth ever since—that is, until the past fifty years or so. The change began in 1967. That was the year an entire generation—the Baby Boom generation—was profoundly affected by a new way of looking at reality. That was the year our culture began to abandon objective truth in favor of feelings and subjective experience.

Why was 1967 so significant? That was the year Dr. Timothy Leary told the thirty thousand gathered for the first Human Be-In in San Francisco's Golden Gate Park to "turn on, tune in, and drop out." The year before, Leary had begun touring the country, presenting a psychedelic light-and-sound show he called "The Death of the Mind" meant to simulate the experience of being on LSD and to encourage audiences to experiment with the drug as a means of detaching themselves from cultural conventions and objective truth.

Leary's message in January 1967 was followed by the "Summer of Love," when hundreds of thousands of hippies converged on cities across North America and Europe. The biggest gathering was in San Francisco's Haight-Ashbury district, where one hundred thousand hippies staged a mass experiment with psychedelic drugs, acid rock music, promiscuous sex, and political rebellion. Years later, *Time* magazine said that the overriding theme of the "Summer of Love" was "trust your feelings."[8]

In August 1967, the Beatles met with the Indian guru Maharishi Mahesh Yogi and began preaching Eastern religion to an entire generation. Those three events—the tours of Timothy Leary, the drug-drenched "Summer of Love," and the Beatles' "magical mystery tour" message of drug trips and Eastern mysticism—infected the sixties generation with these deadly messages: Turn off your mind. Abandon objective truth. Trust your feelings. The events that followed—urban riots, the assassination of Robert F. Kennedy and Martin Luther King, Jr., stagnation in Vietnam, a gas crisis, Watergate—further disillusioned many Baby Boomers. Instead of seeking truth from traditional sources, they embraced the call to make their own feelings the final authority.

A decade later, the George Lucas film *Star Wars* reinforced the message, as the mystical Jedi master Obi-Wan Kenobi advised a young, uncertain Luke Skywalker, who was preparing to fire on the Death Star from his aircraft while warding off attacks by other pilots, "Trust your feelings!" Today the hippie generation that bought into that irrational, anti-truth message has turned gray and lives on Social Security—but they have taught this antirational message to their children and grandchildren. The message has spread. It now infects not just a generation, but our entire culture.

"Trust your feelings." What kind of message is that to build a civilization on? If your teenager is going out on a date, would you give that advice? "Have a good time—and whatever you do, don't think! Don't trust your good sense and the godly principles we have taught you. No, trust your feelings!" What loving parent would give such advice to a son or daughter?

Or suppose a driver cuts you off on the freeway—how should you respond? Should you rely on reason and sound thinking? Should you rely on biblical principles of good judgment and self-control? Or should you "trust your feelings"? There's a name for the way people act when they trust their feelings on the freeway. It's called road rage.

And what if your spouse came to you and confessed, "I've been having lustful feelings for someone at the office. I think I should change jobs and remove any temptation to be unfaithful." What would you tell your spouse? "Oh, no, honey! Don't trust your thinking! Trust your feelings!" What sane wife or husband would ever say such a thing?

Yet the notion that we should trust our feelings is promoted as wisdom in our culture today. Many people from the "trust your feelings" generation are now political leaders, business executives, journalists, TV producers, and university professors. They are relying on their feelings to make decisions and promote ideas that should require logic, rational thinking, and a concern for others.

If the year 1517 marked the beginning of Western civilization, it might well be that 1967 marked, if not the end of Western civilization, then perhaps the beginning of the end.

"THEY HAD DEHUMANIZED ME"

While the sixties culture promoted "free love" and self-fulfillment, this focus on individuals doing whatever made them happy also began the marginalization of those who remained committed to biblical truth. In her 1906 book *The Friends of Voltaire*, Evelyn Beatrice Hall summed up the attitude of the French philosopher Voltaire toward his ideological opponents: "I disapprove of what you say, but I will defend to the death your right to say it."[9] In our polarized and violent age, the notion of actually *defending* the free-speech rights of our opponents seems almost quaint. Yet that is the *only* way truth can be respected and protected. We must all be free to speak, and we must all be willing to listen, otherwise what we call "civilization" will dissolve into chaos and madness. In order to have a civilization, we must be civilized and civil to one another.

Unfortunately, the April 2017 attack on Heather Mac Donald's free speech rights at Claremont McKenna College is hardly an isolated incident. In fact, violent leftist assaults on free speech are becoming an epidemic on campuses from coast to coast. Not only truth, but academic freedom and equality are on the scaffold, facing execution, as lawless protestors roam our university campuses, armed with rocks, bats, and pepper spray.

We saw it multiple times at the University of California, Berkeley, home of the so-called "Free Speech Movement" of the mid-1960s. The group behind the 2017 Berkeley riots—which occurred both on campus and in the city proper—calls itself "Antifa," which is short for "anti-fascist." The group members gained prominence as the shock troops of the #Resist movement that hopes to reverse the election of President Trump. On Inauguration Day, January 20, 2017, Antifa rioters were on the streets of the nation's capital, battling police, torching trash cans and automobiles, and destroying shop windows with rocks, bricks, and chunks of pavement.

In early 2017, Antifa riots broke out at the Berkeley campus as rioters sought to shut down an appearance by a libertarian speaker with whom they disagreed. An estimated 150 black-clad rioters among the crowd of 1,500 student protesters threw fireworks, Molotov cocktails, bricks, and rocks. They set fires near the bookstore, smashed windows of the student union, tore down part of the construction site of a new dorm, vandalized a downtown bank branch and other storefronts, and assaulted bystanders. During this rampage of violence and destruction, Berkeley police stood by, obeying orders from higher-ups to maintain a "hands off" approach.[10] One young woman wearing a red Trump-style hat was being interviewed by CNN when an Antifa thug called out to her. When she turned, he shot pepper spray in her eyes.[11]

In April, a Patriots Day rally in a Berkeley city park turned violent as Antifa protesters clashed with Trump supporters. During the standoff, a masked man attacked Trump supporter Sean Stiles with a steel U-shaped bike lock. The vicious blow knocked Stiles to the ground, where he sat stunned and bleeding profusely from his head. The attacker melted into the crowd, but video of the incident helped police identify the man. The alleged attacker, a community college philosophy professor, was charged with felony assault with a deadly weapon.[12]

Berkeley's Antifa group promised to respond with more violence if conservative commentator Ann Coulter was allowed to speak on campus in April. Three days later, the university said Coulter's appearance was off because it was unable to provide a secure location for Coulter's speech. Police also said they could not ensure the safety of the speaker, audience, or protesters. After Coulter and others objected, university officials said they had found a secure location for her talk and would reschedule her appearance for early May—on a day with no classes when many students wouldn't be on campus. In effect, city and university officials allowed Antifa to deprive Coulter and the conservative students of their First Amendment rights through what is called a "heckler's veto."

Next, we move up the coast from Berkeley, California, to Olympia, Washington, and the campus of Evergreen State College. There, in April 2017, a planning committee from the 4,089-student college called for a "Day of Absence" when white students, white faculty, and white staff were encouraged to remain off campus with the administration's approval.

One Evergreen professor, biologist Bret Weinstein, refused to participate and announced he would be in his classroom as scheduled. Several weeks later Weinstein—who called himself a "deeply progressive person" and a Bernie Sanders supporter during the 2016 primaries—had his classroom invaded by about fifty screaming, cursing students who accused him of being a racist and calling people of color useless. When protesters armed themselves with baseball bats, Weinstein prudently decided to move his next class to a public park in downtown Olympia.

The day after confronting Weinstein in his classroom, the protesters intimidated the college president into giving them everything they demanded, including free pizza and complete amnesty for homework assigned during the protests. They even demanded that the college president admit and renounce the sin of racism. The frightened president agreed to publicly disavow his "white supremacy." At one point he raised his hand to try to get a word in. A female student jeered at him for "pointing fingers," and the president apologized, put his hand in his pocket, and shut up.

As the Evergreen crisis continued, some student radicals began prowling the campus with baseball bats, saying they were hunting for white supremacists. Students who had refused to go along with the radical uprising feared for their safety, prompting the administration to send out an e-mail to remind students that "the use of bats or similar instruments is not productive."[13]

Some five months after the student uprising began, a college spokesperson announced that, during the spring and summer quarters, 80 of the 180 student protesters had received "sanctions ranging from formal warnings, community service and probation, to suspension." The college did not disclose the exact number of suspensions.[14]

We move from the Pacific Northwest to New England, where a conservative student group at Middlebury College in Vermont invited libertarian author Charles Alan Murray to speak on campus. As soon as the Murray lecture was announced, leftist students and alumni began to mobilize against the event. One letter, signed by more than 450 alumni, demanded the invitation be rescinded, adding, "This is not an issue of freedom of speech. Why has such a person been granted a platform at Middlebury?"

Totalitarian leftists often claim that no one has a First Amendment right to spout hate speech. By their definition, any speech they disapprove of is automatically hate speech. They have reserved unto themselves the authority to deem whose speech is protected by the First Amendment and whose is not.

Murray arrived to deliver his talk on March 2, 2017. His host and interviewer for the event was Middlebury professor Allison Stanger. At the very outset, protesters began to heckle and chant, "Your message is hatred, we cannot tolerate it!" and "Charles Murray go away, Middlebury says no way!" So Murray and Stanger moved from that building to a secret location in the McCullough Student Center and conducted the talk via a closed-circuit broadcast.

Later, as Murray and Stanger were leaving the student center, they found themselves and their car surrounded by protesters, many of them wearing masks (masks are usually a sign of violent intentions, because the maskwearers don't want to be identified). As Murray and Stanger tried to enter the car, Stanger shielded Murray (who is in his midseventies) from the protesters. The protesters grabbed Stanger by the hair and arms, twisting her neck. Other protesters jumped onto the hood of the car and rocked it back and forth. Still others threw down a barrier in front of the car so that it couldn't be driven away.[15]

Murray and Stanger escaped from the protesters, and Stanger was later hospitalized with a concussion and neck injuries. Allison Stanger, a liberal political science professor at Middlebury who believes in the First Amendment, has called that day, "the saddest day of my life." She wrote in a Facebook post:

> I want you to know what it feels like to look out at a sea of students yelling obscenities at other members of my beloved community. . . .
>
> What alarmed me most, however, was what I saw in student eyes from up on that stage. Those who wanted the event to take place made eye contact with me. Those intent on disrupting it steadfastly refused to do so. It was clear to me that they had effectively dehumanized me. They couldn't look me in the eye, because if they had, they would have seen another human being. There is a lot to be angry about in America today, but nothing good ever comes from demonizing our brothers and sisters.[16]

Unlike Claremont McKenna, U.C. Berkeley, and Evergreen, which delayed student discipline, Middlebury College addressed the violence immediately. The school enforced disciplinary action against sixty-seven students who took part in the violent student uprising.

"STOP THE EXECUTION!"

Kimberley Strassel writes the Potomac Watch column for the *Wall Street Journal* and is the author of *The Intimidation Game: How the Left Is Silencing Free Speech*. In an April 2017 speech at Hillsdale College in Michigan, she offered a simple yet profound analogy of the three views of free speech in America today.

"I have three kids, ages twelve, nine, and five," she said. "They are your average, normal kids—which means they live to annoy the heck out of each other."

One night during dinner, the twelve-year-old son was bothering the five-year-old daughter, and the little girl was so frustrated that she told him, "You need to stop talking—*forever*." That statement ignited a debate among the children about free speech rights. Ms. Strassel asked her children to explain, one at a time, what "free speech" meant to him or her.

The twelve-year-old son had recently studied the Constitution in school and talked about James Madison, the First Amendment, and the meaning of the phrase "Congress shall make no law."

The nine-year-old daughter confessed that she didn't understand all the terminology that her older brother used, but to her, free speech meant "there should never be any restrictions on *anything* that *anybody* says, *anytime* or *anywhere*." She concluded that her brother and sister should listen more to what *she* had to say.

Next, the five-year-old glared at her siblings and said, "Free speech is that you can say what you want—as long as I like it."

Strassel experienced a moment of great clarity and insight just then. She realized that her three children represented the three prevailing political viewpoints in our society today. Her twelve-year-old son was a constitutional conservative. Her middle child was a libertarian. And her youngest child was "a socialist with totalitarian tendencies."[17]

This is what we are up against in America today. It is harder than ever to communicate the truth to a society where totalitarian socialists with the emotional maturity and impulse control of a five-year-old have veto power over what can be said in our institutions of higher learning. On our university campuses, and across our culture, truth is on the scaffold.

You and I must stand between the totalitarian socialists and the endangered truth. We must be ready to shout, "Stop the execution! Let truth live!" If we let freedom and truth be put to death in our generation, what hope will our children and grandchildren have?

Yes, we must stop the execution of truth—even though we know full well where the mob will turn its rage next.

3

WHAT AMERICA IS—
AND ISN'T

A NUMBER OF YEARS AGO, actor Tom Hanks spoke with a magazine interviewer about World War II and America's conflict with Japan. He said that Americans hated the Japanese people because of their racial characteristics and because the Japanese people "believed in different gods." (I won't repeat the racially disparaging terms Hanks used.) The Japanese, he said, "were out to kill us because our way of living was different. We, in turn, wanted to annihilate them because they were different."[1]

In other words, Hanks wants us to know that America was a racist nation during World War II, and we fought against the Japanese because of our racial hatred toward them. Then Hanks went on to ask, "Does that sound familiar, by any chance, to what's going on today?" So in Hanks's worldview, America is still a racist nation, and our war against the Taliban, Al Qaeda, ISIS, and other terrorist organizations is *also* motivated by racial and religious hatred.

Hanks seems to forget the fact that both America's war against

Japan and America's war on terror were triggered by unprovoked attacks against our nation. Japan attacked Pearl Harbor on December 7, 1941—and Al Qaeda, aided by the Taliban in Afghanistan who shielded bin Laden, attacked New York's World Trade Center and the Pentagon in Washington, DC, on September 11, 2001. Immediately after Japan surrendered in 1945, America—this "racist" nation that Hanks claimed wanted to annihilate the Japanese simply because they were different—spent billions of American taxpayer dollars to feed the war-ravaged Japanese people and rebuild their nation. And even as the war on terror goes on, American taxpayers are spending billions of dollars building roads, schools, and infrastructure in Afghanistan.

If America is truly a racist nation, as Mr. Hanks claims, why are we spending so much time and treasure trying to rebuild the societies of these people we supposedly hate? If our goal was to annihilate the people of Japan and Afghanistan, as this actor claims, why does all the evidence scream that he is wrong?

In this interview, Tom Hanks reflects many of the views of the Hollywood left, which often operates on a set of assumptions—call them dogmas—that include:

- America is no better than any other country. In fact, America is a racist country that neglects the poor and exploits other nations, which actually makes it worse than most other countries.
- The term *American exceptionalism* is a code for American arrogance and chauvinism. In America, the police victimize blacks, whites victimize Latinos, men victimize women, straights victimize gays, and Christians victimize Muslims.

- America is a greedy country that became wealthy by cheating and exploiting the rest of the world.
- America's history of slavery and segregation proves that America does not deserve to hold a place of moral leadership in the world.

If you attend a university, listen to the Hollywood left, or tune in to progressive commentators in the news media, you may find that these dogmas underlie much of what you see and hear. This is the filter through which many leftists perceive reality.

But these dogmas are not reality. These dogmas do not tell the truth about America.

The United States fought a costly, bloody Civil War to destroy the racist institution of slavery. And America spent the next hundred years battling racial segregation—albeit imperfectly—and seeking to extend the blessings of liberty to people of all races. The rejection of racism is essential to who we are as Americans. It's stated plainly in the Declaration of Independence: "We hold these truths to be self-evident, that all men are created equal, that they are endowed by their Creator with certain unalienable Rights, that among these are Life, Liberty and the pursuit of Happiness."

No other nation on earth has been so welcoming and generous toward people of other cultures, races, and religions. No other nation has lent more assistance to nations in times of crisis or need, asking nothing in return. No other nation has spent more blood and treasure to liberate other people and nations from tyranny. No other nation in the world is more ethnically and racially diverse. And even though we have not yet solved all of our racial divisions or healed all of our racial wounds, I don't believe any other nation on earth is more ethnically and racially harmonious than America.

ONLY IN AMERICA

David Horowitz—a former radical leftist turned conservative activist—discussed the notion that America is a racist country:

> This accusation is one that so-called progressives regularly make against a country that outlaws racial discrimination, has twice elected a black president, had two black secretaries of state, three black national security advisors and two successive black attorneys general. . . . The claim that America is a white supremacist nation is . . . an act of hostility towards blacks, who enjoy opportunities and rights as Americans that are greater than those of any other country under the sun.[2]

America still has many unsolved racial problems—but if you want to see far worse racial strife, I could take you to parts of Asia, Africa, Latin America, or the Arab world and show you racial hatred, unrest, and violence that would sicken your soul. I could show you places where human slavery is still practiced in the twenty-first century. In fact, according to the global advocacy organization Free the Slaves, there are more human beings in chains of slavery today than there were at the time of the American Civil War. The UN International Labor Organization estimates that there are 21 million people worldwide who are trapped in involuntary servitude, sex slavery, or child slavery.[3]

According to a statistical analysis of data compiled by the World Values Survey, America is among the least racist, most tolerant societies in the world. From 2010 to 2014, the survey asked people in more than eighty nations who they would not want to live next to as neighbors. Among Americans, only 5 percent responded "people of a different race." Compare that with the most racist nations in the world, according to the survey: Libya (54 percent), India (43.6 percent), Palestine (44 percent), Lebanon (36.3 percent), Bahrain (31.1 percent), the Philippines (30.6 percent), South Korea (29.6 percent), Kuwait (28.1 percent), and South Africa (19.6 percent).[4]

This information often comes as a shock to Americans, who have been bombarded with anti-American propaganda from the mainstream media. Conflict sells newspapers, keeps people tuned in to TV news, and heats up social media sites (where increasing numbers of Americans now get their news). Racial warfare is a ratings hot button. So most Americans, and especially liberal Americans, are inclined to think the worst of their own nation's record on race.

But the truth is that America fights for fairness and justice, gives generously, and accepts people who are yearning to be free. That's why millions line up every year to come to America. That's why I was one of those waiting in line to realize my own American dream.

Only in America do you find the principles of freedom of religion, freedom of speech, freedom of the press, freedom to peaceably assemble, and the right to petition the government outlined in the first statement of the Bill of Rights. No other nation in the world guarantees these five essential freedoms in its founding documents.

PERFECT PRINCIPLES FOR IMPERFECT PEOPLE

Unfortunately, we Americans have grown tragically complacent about our rights and freedoms. We think that the rampant abuses and injustices we see in other parts of the world could never happen here. I wish that were true, but I know it's a false hope.

In 1852, abolitionist Wendell Phillips told the Massachusetts Anti-Slavery Society, "Eternal vigilance is the price of liberty; power is ever stealing from the many to the few. The manna of popular liberty must be gathered each day or it is rotten." He added that one of the greatest dangers to liberty is the complacency that develops when we become prosperous and comfortable. That's when we face the greatest danger of allowing liberty to "be smothered in material prosperity."[5]

We the people need to understand what America is—and isn't.

America is not a piece of real estate, a geographical region bordered by Canada, Mexico, and two oceans.

America is not the US government.

America is not even the American people.

America is *a set of ideas*, embodied in the founding documents of America—the Declaration of Independence and the United States Constitution. When government officials and military personnel take the oath of their office or profession, they do not swear to defend American land, the American government, or the American people. They swear to protect and defend *the Constitution of the United States*.

That's significant. That should make us pause and realize what the name *America* really means. It should make us realize what it means to *be* an American. To be an American means so much more than simply being born on the soil of the United States. To be an American means to believe in, support, and defend the truths and principles embodied in the Declaration of Independence and the Constitution.

Now, let's be completely candid about American history. The

men who wrote and signed the Declaration and the Constitution were not perfect men. Some did not fully live up to the ideals contained in the documents they were signing. Take, for example, Thomas Jefferson, the man who conceived and wrote the Declaration of Independence.

He was born in 1743, the son of a wealthy Virginia farmer, Peter Jefferson. When Thomas Jefferson was fourteen, his father died, leaving him five thousand acres of land. His father also bequeathed about 50 slaves to him; years later Jefferson inherited another 135 slaves from his father-in-law. A brilliant young man, Jefferson was fluent in Latin, Greek, French, Italian, and Spanish. At the College of William and Mary, he studied the writings of the English empiricists—Francis Bacon, Isaac Newton, and John Locke. He developed a deep understanding of many subjects, ranging from mathematics and science to philosophy, literature, and ethics. He completed his chosen course of studies in only two years, after which he was tutored in the study of law and was admitted to the Virginia bar in 1767. He wrote the Declaration of Independence in 1776, when he was just thirty-three years old.

Despite his many accomplishments, Thomas Jefferson was a deeply conflicted man. He was a slaveholder who believed in his conscience that slavery was morally wrong. When Jefferson wrote those beautiful words of the Declaration of Independence—"that all men are created equal, that they are endowed by their Creator with certain unalienable Rights"—he fully believed them, and he knew in his heart that those words applied to people of every race and color, including the slaves who served him on his plantation. Slavery was the source of Jefferson's wealth—and a direct contradiction of the Enlightenment ideals he believed in. When Jefferson wrote those phrases into the Declaration of Independence, his conscience condemned him. Yet he could not or would not free his slaves.

Jefferson knew that slavery was a moral stain on his nation. He feared (and rightly so) that slavery would someday tear America apart. In his book *Notes on the State of Virginia* (1781), he wrote,

> Can the liberties of a nation be thought secure when we have removed their only firm basis, a conviction in the minds of the people that these liberties are of the gift of God? That they are not to be violated but with his wrath? Indeed I tremble for my country when I reflect that God is just: that his justice cannot sleep for ever. . . . The spirit of the master is abating, that of the slave rising from the dust.[6]

Jefferson even used his legal skills to defend slaves who sued in court to be emancipated. He once defended a slave named Samuel Howell, and in his argument before the court he said, "All men are born free [and] everyone comes into the world with a right to his own person." But the judge interrupted Jefferson's argument and ruled against him and his client. After the trial, Jefferson gave money to Howell out of his own pocket—money Howell later used to escape to freedom.[7]

Though Jefferson was conscientiously opposed to slavery, he continued to own slaves. Historian Andrew Burstein offers an explanation of this self-contradiction: "Jefferson saw African-Americans as noble human beings. In the abstract, he could appreciate the African-American's humanity. . . . Jefferson wanted slaves to have decent lives. He wanted to be the best slaveholder in America. . . . He did not think that America was politically ready [to abolish slavery]. . . . Jefferson . . . was a political pragmatist."[8]

Slavery was, is, and always will be evil—and Jefferson clearly said so in his book and in the words of the Declaration of Independence. His view of his own role as a slave owner was distorted by the culture in which he lived. Jefferson was born into a world in which slavery was the norm—it was all he had ever known. But he wanted to be a kind and enlightened slave master. He rationalized that his kindness to his slaves somehow compensated for keeping his fellow man in bondage, violating the noble words of the Declaration.

And this is important to understand: If you and I had been born into a slave-holding culture, our view of slavery might have been as distorted as Jefferson's. Our culture shapes our thinking.

But moral principles are unyielding, and Jefferson's failure to free his own slaves is a blot on his legacy. He had a moral obligation to live his life according to the truth he had received. He wrote beautiful words about equality and liberty, words that still inspire and instruct us today. Those words inspired thousands of white abolitionists to fight for the dignity and liberation of their black brothers and sisters. The nation fought a civil war because of those words.

Those beautiful words did not benefit his own slaves, however. Jefferson may have been a kind and enlightened slave master. But he was a slave master nonetheless.

Thomas Jefferson is an example to you and me of why it is so important to live the truth, to obey the principles we say we believe and to do what's right, even when there's a price to pay. The perfect principles of the Declaration of Independence were delivered to us by imperfect men like Thomas Jefferson. The fact that Jefferson didn't live up to them does not invalidate those principles. In fact, it should make us want to live up to them all the more.

All too many opinion leaders, both in America and in other countries, blame America for all that is wrong in the world—for terrorism, for global tensions, for poverty around the globe, for chants of "Death to America" in Iran, Syria, and other Islamic nations. America has never been, nor ever will be, a perfect country. But there are not many other countries where people line up for days or weeks to get in—and I can think of no other nation in the world where millions of people sneak in illegally every year. If America is the source of all the world's evils and ills, why are so many people willing to risk everything, even their lives and their children's lives, to get here?

I know why people want to come to America. I know because I was not born in the United States, but I dreamed of living in freedom as an American. When I became a citizen, I did not become a hyphenated American. I simply became an American. I love America's exceptionalism, and I have spent much of my career as a speaker and author proclaiming it and defending it.

The nation I love, the nation that adopted me, is facing dark times. For many people, the American dream—the idea of being rewarded for hard work and ingenuity—is becoming a nightmare. Liberty is in decline; oppression is on the rise. The national debt has reached a frighteningly unsustainable level, threatening to crash the global economy. School shootings, race wars, murders, and suicides are epidemic in our society.

Everywhere we hear people pleading for peace—peace in their communities, peace in the Middle East, peace of mind—yet there is no peace. Every Christmas, we hear the stories of the angels announcing, "Peace on earth, good will toward men." And every new year seems to bring more war, more terror, and less peace than the year before.

Herein lies the truth that the so-called "wise men" of our times have no wish to hear: There can be no peace without the Prince of Peace at the center of our national life and our society. And since our governments, courts, and educational institutions have eliminated God from public life, it stands to reason that peace will only become more and more elusive with each passing year.

The Bill of Rights enshrines the God-given right of all people to practice any religion: "Congress shall make no law respecting an establishment of religion, or prohibiting the free exercise thereof." I love the system of government that our founding fathers gave us. Only by guaranteeing freedom of thought, speech, conscience, and religion *for all* do we insure our own freedom.

I am not proposing that we impose a theocracy on America. I do not wish to see the establishment of a state religion.

But there are eternal principles that we disobey at our peril, moral principles that we derive from the Judeo-Christian Bible, principles our founding fathers believed in and built our nation upon. These principles are perfectly compatible with our United States Constitution, and our nation observed these principles during the first two centuries or so of its existence. America began veering away from these principles during the latter part of the twentieth century, but it's not too late to correct our course—not yet. God offers us a choice: accept His moral principles and the blessings that come with them—or reject them and risk losing our liberty.

Americans have debated the limits of government's involvement in religion for a long time. In 1854, the House Judiciary Committee studied the question of whether the establishment clause of the First Amendment prohibited the service of chaplains in Congress, the army, and the navy. The conclusion of the committee:

> The ecclesiastical and civil powers have been, and should continue to be, entirely divorced from each other. But we beg leave to rescue ourselves from the imputation of asserting that religion is not needed to the safety of civil society. [Religion] must be considered as the foundation on which the whole structure rests. Laws will not have permanence or power without the sanction of religious sentiment—without a firm belief that there is a Power above us that will reward our virtues and punish our vices. In this age there can be no substitute for Christianity. . . . That was the religion of the founders of the republic, and they expected it to remain the religion of their descendants.[9]

Today, many secularists and atheists try to sell the notion that America was *not* built on a foundation of Christian morality and the Christian religion. For example, the Freedom from Religion Foundation website features an article that begins, "The Christian Right is trying to rewrite the history of the United States, as part of their campaign to force their religion on others who ask merely to be left alone. According to this Orwellian revision, the Founding Fathers of this country were pious Christians who wanted the United States to be a Christian nation, with laws that favored Christians and Christianity."[10]

The author of those words is simply wrong on several counts. For one thing, we Christians are not trying to "force" our religion on anyone—that would be a *violation* of the Lord's great commission and an *affront* to our religion. The Christian gospel is an invitation, not an imposition. Nor do we seek to make evangelical Christianity the state-established religion of the United States.

And the author of the Freedom from Religion Foundation article is also mistaken regarding the beliefs of the founding fathers. Let me cite a few examples:

Daniel Webster served in the United States Senate and as Secretary of State, and he was nicknamed "The Defender of the Constitution." He said, "Our ancestors established their system of government on morality and religious sentiment. . . . Whatever makes men good Christians, makes them good citizens."[11] He also said, "The Christian religion, its general principles, must ever be regarded among us as the foundation of civil society."[12]

John Adams was a signer of the Declaration of Independence and one of only two signers of the Bill of Rights; he succeeded George Washington as the second president of the United States. In a letter to Thomas Jefferson, June 28, 1813, Adams wrote, "The general principles on which the fathers achieved independence, were . . . the general principles of Christianity, in which all those sects were united, and the general principles of English and American liberty. . . . Those general principles of Christianity are as eternal and immutable as the existence and attributes of God; and . . . those principles of liberty are as unalterable as human nature."[13] On another occasion, he wrote, "Without religion, this world would be something not fit to be mentioned in polite company—I mean Hell."[14]

And George Washington, "The Father of Our Country," when he was commander-in-chief of the Continental Army at Valley Forge, issued an order on May 2, 1778, that Christian worship services be performed every Sunday at 11 o'clock, and that officers set a good example to the enlisted men by attending regularly. He added, "While we are zealously performing the duties of good Citizens and soldiers we certainly ought not to be inattentive to the higher duties of Religion—To the distinguished Character of Patriot, it should be our highest Glory to add the more distinguished Character of Christian."[15]

In 1779, about midway through the American Revolutionary War, General Washington was approached by a delegation of the Delaware tribe of Native American people. The Delawares wanted to make a pact of friendship with the government of the new American nation, and they wanted to learn the Christian religion. So Washington, as commander-in-chief of the Continental Army, spoke to the Delaware delegation on May 12, 1779, and he said this about the Christian faith: "You do well to wish to learn our arts and ways of life and above all—the religion of Jesus Christ. These will make you a greater and happier people than you are. Congress will do everything they can to assist you in this wise intention; and to tie the knot of friendship and union so fast—that nothing shall ever be able to loose it."[16]

The founding fathers saw no conflict between religious liberty and the fact that America was founded on the principles of the Christian faith. They wanted nothing to do with a state-sponsored, state-imposed church, such as the Church of England. But they knew that the American people needed to practice the principles of the Christian faith, and the American government needed to be founded on those same principles. No American would be forced to profess any religious beliefs or belong to any religious denomination—an atheist would have nothing to fear. But it was commonly understood that America could only thrive and remain free so long as its people, on the whole, remained dependent upon Almighty God.

What I have described to you is America 1.0, the original America, the America that millions of older Americans reflect on with nostalgia. It's the land they were born in, were raised in, and grew up in. And these older Americans feel a deep sense of disappointment that, over the past few decades, America 1.0 has disappeared. It has been replaced by America 2.0, a secularist America that denies our nation's rich history of faith. Many Americans are saddened and angry that their children and grandchildren are growing up in a very different America—an America that no longer values biblical principles and morality.

I came to this country from a land of Islamic and socialist tyranny because I longed to be free. In Egypt, I read the writings of America's founders and dreamed of breathing the air of freedom that was purchased with the blood of American patriots. I know I speak for millions of legal immigrants, plus millions of Americans whose ancestors emigrated to America decades or centuries ago. Many of us still value the America that once was, the America that could be once more.

We want the America that feared God.

We want the America whose foundation was the Bible.

We want the America that expected its leaders to be people of sound moral character and strong principles.

America is in a race to the depths of immorality, insolvency, and moral insanity. But America's descent can be halted and reversed.

It's up to us. It's up to you and me, and all others who claim to follow Christ as Lord and Savior. By the end of this book, you will know what must be done to reverse our downward course.

SECULARISM:
THE ENEMY WITHIN

UNION ARMY GENERAL George McClellan was admired by his men, who nicknamed him "Young Napoleon." He gave his soldiers the training, equipment, and encouragement they needed to win on the battlefield, yet he was reluctant to commit his troops to battle.

He led the Peninsula Campaign against Richmond, the Confederate capital. Historians generally agree that he would have won if he had taken the battle to the enemy. But Confederate commander Joseph E. Johnston moved his meager forces around, tricking McClellan into thinking he faced overwhelming numbers. McClellan cautiously delayed and delayed, allowing the Confederates time to reinforce themselves.

McClellan also delayed at the Battle of Seven Pines, allowing the army of General Robert E. Lee to repeatedly assault and wear down McClellan's forces. The Confederates had figured out how to use McClellan's caution against him.

At Antietam on September 17, 1862—the bloodiest day of

the Civil War—McClellan's excess of caution again prevented the Union from achieving a decisive victory. He could have cut off the Confederates' retreat and shortened the war. Instead, he pulled back.

President Lincoln needed generals who would fight. In November 1862, Lincoln relieved McClellan of command.

Back home in New Jersey, pondering his sacking by Lincoln, McClellan became increasingly bitter. He had once admired President Lincoln, but he soon came to despise him. Finally, McClellan knew what he had to do.

He ran for the Democratic nomination for president—and won. Next, he opposed his former commander-in-chief, Abraham Lincoln, in the 1864 general election. Though he was personally pro-war, McClellan resented President Lincoln so much that he ran on the Democrats' anti-war platform, which pledged to negotiate a compromise peace with the slaveholding South. Most pundits and political observers—and even President Lincoln himself—predicted that McClellan would win.

Had General McClellan won the election and pursued the Democratic Party's peace plan, the United States might still be divided to this day—and who knows how long slavery would have continued? But the voters rejected McClellan and re-elected Lincoln.

Imagine the loneliness of Abraham Lincoln in the fall of 1864 as the Civil War raged on and one of his own generals campaigned against him. Mr. Lincoln fought for the Union, fought against slavery, fought on two fronts. He fought the enemy without—the Confederate Army—on the battlefield. And he fought the enemy within—General McClellan—on the political front.

Today we, too, must confront the enemy within our nation— the enemy called secularism.

SECULAR FUNDAMENTALISM

In recent years, a new term has entered the English language: *secular fundamentalism*. Secularists, agnostics, and atheists object to that term because they think of themselves as enlightened freethinkers. Nothing could be more insulting to a secularist than to be labeled a "fundamentalist."

That's why one of the leading secularists in America, Sam Harris, author of *The End of Faith*, posted a video at the Big Think website entitled "What Is Secular Fundamentalism?" He said, "This whole idea of 'secular fundamentalism' or 'atheist dogmatism'—this is really a play on words. There's nothing that you have to accept as dogma. There's nothing you have to accept on insufficient evidence in order to reject the biblical God, or in order to reject the idea that the Qur'an or the Bible is the perfect Word of God."[1]

It's not surprising that Sam Harris shudders at the notion of being called a secular fundamentalist. In his worldview, there's nothing worse than a fundamentalist—so he shrugs off the term as a "play on words," mere verbal trickery on the part of religious people to point the finger of blame back at atheists. But "secular fundamentalism" is no mere play on words. It is a real phenomenon, and Mr. Harris is one of its adherents, whether he likes to think so or not.

The Urban Dictionary defines *Secular-Fundamentalism* as "the adherence to anti-religious ideology that militantly ridicules, mocks, scorns and satirizes the idea of the existence of a deity or deities and/or religion." Secular fundamentalists call for "religion to [be] removed from public life" and "regard religion as inherently harmful."[2] Someone has also defined *fundamentalism*

as "a singular outlook in a pluralistic world"—and that definition certainly applies to secular fundamentalists. They believe
their view—secularism, the absence of all reference to religion—is
the only right view, and they seek to impose it on the rest of us.
Here are five "case studies" that reveal core principles of secular
fundamentalism:

1. *The case of the deadly proposition.* Sam Harris, the atheist
    who said that the concept of secular fundamentalism is
    nothing more than a "play on words," made a statement
    in his book *The End of Faith* that stirred up a huge contro-
    versy: "Some propositions are so dangerous that it may even
    be ethical to kill people for believing them." This resulted in
    a Twitter storm of accusations and name-calling, in which
    Harris was unfortunately (and, I think, unfairly) labeled
    "a genocidal fascist maniac." In his blog, he complained
    (with good reason) that his critics had taken his words out
    of context. I want to be fair to him, so I will quote his words
    from *The End of Faith*, using the same context he provides
    in his 2014 blog post "Response to Controversy":

    > The link between belief and behavior raises the
    > stakes considerably. Some propositions are so
    > dangerous that it may even be ethical to kill people
    > for believing them. This may seem an extraordinary
    > claim, but it merely enunciates an ordinary fact
    > about the world in which we live. Certain beliefs
    > place their adherents beyond the reach of every
    > peaceful means of persuasion, while inspiring them
    > to commit acts of extraordinary violence against

others. There is, in fact, no talking to some people.
If they cannot be captured, and they often cannot,
otherwise tolerant people may be justified in killing
them in self-defense. This is what the United States
attempted in Afghanistan, and it is what we and
other Western powers are bound to attempt, at
an even greater cost to ourselves and to innocents
abroad, elsewhere in the Muslim world. We will
continue to spill blood in what is, at bottom,
a war of ideas.[3]

I understand what Mr. Harris is saying. Ideas drive behavior. Islamist ideology, derived from specific passages of the Qur'an, motivates the torture, terror, and slaughter being committed daily by Islamic fundamentalists. Extremists are prompted by their ideas to kill innocent people, and their behavior is an existential threat to our civilization.

But Mr. Harris is wrong—*fundamentally* wrong—in saying that, in the war on terror, the Western nations are killing radical Islamists for what they *believe*. When a Western soldier takes the life of a radical Islamist terrorist, that killing is justified by what the Islamist *does* (killing and terrorizing innocent people), not by what the Islamist *believes* (Islamic fundamentalism). This may seem like a fine distinction to Mr. Harris, but it is not.

Even in context, Mr. Harris's statement that "it may even be ethical to kill people for believing" certain ideas is dangerous. Once we accept that notion as an ethical principle, many currently "unthinkable" acts become thinkable, including executing people for various "thought crimes," and even for being Christians, Orthodox Jews, or Tea Party members—for holding any beliefs that the State thinks might conceivably make those people "dangerous." Any secularist who claims that it is ethical to kill people because of what they believe is a fundamentalist.

2. *The case of the preaching governor.* This is a small matter, but I think it says a lot about the mind-set of the secular fundamentalists in the media. During the 2016 Republican presidential primary, I noticed that the commentators on various TV news shows would refer to former governor Mike Huckabee as a "former Baptist minister" or "preacher-turned-politician," sometimes without ever mentioning that he had served more than two full terms as governor of Arkansas (prior to being twice elected, he completed the unexpired term of his disgraced predecessor). Even though Governor Huckabee had not been a full-time minister since 1992, that was how these news commentators chose to label him.

This was not an overt attack, but a subtle way of diminishing Governor Huckabee's qualifications as a competent chief executive. Secular fundamentalists are not overly fond of Baptist ministers—and these media figures were sending out a subliminal message to their viewers: *He's not qualified to be president—and if you don't look out, he'll impose his religion on you.* This is a clear case of secular fundamentalism in the news media.

3. *The case of the censored chaplain.* Chaplain Kenneth Reyes of Joint Base Elmendorf-Richardson in Alaska had a regular

column on the base website called "Chaplain's Corner." One of his articles was entitled "No Atheists in Foxholes." This prompted a complaint from a small secular fundamentalist group that has misnamed itself the Military Religious Freedom Foundation. The group is devoted to preventing Christian military personnel from openly practicing or speaking about their faith. The head of the group complained that Chaplain Reyes had used "bigoted, religious supremacist" language in his "anti-secular diatribe."[4]

In fact, Chaplain Reyes had simply told the story of the origin of the famous saying, "There are no atheists in foxholes." (It was coined during World War II by Chaplain William Cummings, during the Japanese siege of Corregidor when he noticed how many atheists had begun attending his services.) The base commander surrendered to the atheist pressure group and took the article down. The American Center for Law and Justice intervened, informed the air force that the chaplain had a legal and constitutional right to post that article, and the air force reposted the article on the base website.[5] But the secular fundamentalists of the Military Religious Freedom Foundation still continue their relentless attacks against Christianity and religious liberty.

4. *The case of the college student rejected for his faith.* Brandon Jenkins wanted to learn how to treat disease through radiation therapy. He applied to the radiation therapy program at Community College of Baltimore County, sent in letters of recommendation, and went through an interview. He later received an e-mail from the director telling him his application had been turned down. Jenkins was shocked to

read this statement from the director: "I understand that religion is a major part of your life and that was evident in your recommendation letters, however, this field is not the place for religion. . . . If you interview in the future, you may want to leave your thoughts and beliefs out of the interview process."

Clearly, a large part of the decision to reject his application was based on his statement in the interview that his Christian faith was important to him. Jenkins was discriminated against by secular fundamentalists at the college who explicitly stated that the field of radiation therapy "is not the place for religion."[6]

5. *The case of the fundamentalist atheist.* Richard Dawkins is an evolutionary biologist and the author of the 2006 book *The God Delusion*. In his book, Professor Dawkins contends that human beings would be happier, less prone to warfare and strife, and generally better off if they didn't believe in God. In that book, Dawkins claims that teaching children about God is a form of psychological "child abuse." He approvingly quotes a colleague, evolutionary psychologist Nicholas Humphrey, who said in a 1997 Oxford lecture:

> Freedom of speech is too precious a freedom to be meddled with. . . . I shall probably shock you when I say it is the purpose of my lecture today to argue in one particular area just the opposite. . . . I am talking about moral and religious education. . . .
>
> Children have a right not to have their minds addled by nonsense. And we as a society have a duty

to protect them from it. So we should no more allow parents to teach their children to believe, for example, in the literal truth of the Bible . . . than we should allow parents to knock their children's teeth out or lock them in a dungeon.[7]

These two respected scientists, Professor Dawkins and Professor Humphrey, openly argue that Christian parents should be forbidden by the state to teach their children about Jesus. These secular elitists have determined that the good news of the gospel cripples a child's mind with religious "dogma and superstition." They sincerely believe that they have more right to determine your child's upbringing than you do yourself. If that is not secular fundamentalism, I don't know what is.

In fact, one of Professor Dawkins's colleagues, Peter Higgs (the famed theorist of the Higgs boson and recipient of the 2013 Nobel Prize in Physics), criticized Dawkins's attacks on religion, telling an interviewer for the Spanish newspaper *El Mundo*, "I think Dawkins himself sometimes adopts a fundamentalist position—but of the opposite kind." Professor Higgs also described his own views, saying, "I am not a believer, but science and religion can be compatible."[8] When Professor Dawkins's own esteemed colleague labels him a secular fundamentalist, I can't help but agree.

Islamic fundamentalists have such an absolute belief in the rightness of their dogmas that they cannot tolerate other religions, they cannot have a dialogue with people who believe differently, they cannot stand the very existence of other views than their own. Secular fundamentalists like Richard Dawkins have a similarly intense revulsion toward religion. They are so utterly convinced of the rightness of their rationalism and atheism that they cannot tolerate religion in any form and cannot allow religious parents to teach their faith to their children. They ridicule, mock, and satirize the idea of God, and they have no empathy whatsoever for the people they have scorned and persecuted. They feel justified and self-righteous.

And that is why, in spite of all their protests against the term, Dawkins and Harris are secular fundamentalists. This term is not a play on words, not a joke. It's a description of a real and dangerous mind-set in our culture.

Anything God has made good can be twisted into something evil by the human mind. God gives us good food, but we pervert it with the sin of gluttony. God gives us the gift of sex and sexuality, but we pervert it with sins of lust and adultery. God gives us faith and the gift of His Word, but we pervert these gifts with man-made legalism, religious arrogance, and intolerance. And God gives us the gift of reason and science, which some have twisted into a justification for intolerant atheism and secularism.

THE GREAT AMERICAN DELUSION

If the founding fathers could visit America today, they wouldn't recognize the nation they established. Where is the industrious, liberty-loving nation for which they risked their lives, fortunes, and sacred honor? It has largely become a place where antisocial behavior is rewarded, where industriousness is penalized, and where our First Amendment freedoms are giving way to political correctness.

For example, in Houston in 2014, the city council and the openly lesbian mayor passed the Houston Equal Rights Ordinance, or HERO, aimed at ending discrimination based on gender identity. Opponents of the ordinance, including many pastors, said the new law would make it impossible to keep predators and voyeurs out of public restrooms. Opponents of the ordinance labeled it "The Sexual Predator Protection Act" and petitioned to have the ordinance placed on the ballot.

The mayor and the city council denied the petition—then went to the extraordinary length of subpoenaing transcripts of sermons by Houston pastors. It was a blatant violation of the First Amendment, intended to intimidate the church and silence dissent. Only when the city's actions ignited a national uproar did city leaders back down. The measure was placed before the voters—and soundly defeated.

Despite the outcome in Houston, those advocating for LGBTQ rights have made major gains in recent years, particularly in their push for same-sex marriage. Proponents point to supposed benefits to society if men could marry men and women could marry women. Same-sex marriage would stimulate the economy (more weddings means more wedding cakes and flowers sold, more hotel rooms booked, more economic activity). Same-sex marriage would make same-sex couples feel accepted—and that would encourage society to be more "inclusive."

Many Christians have been persuaded by the false arguments of the pro-gay-marriage secularist lobby. They reason, *Why should I care if two men or two women want to marry? How does that harm me? Don't I want people to think I'm compassionate?* So the empty arguments have worked, and public opinion has swung in favor of same-sex marriage.

And we are beginning to discover that what is pushed as a commonsense "expansion" of marriage is a lot more costly and destructive than we were led to believe.

FREEDOM UNDER ATTACK

In June 2015, the US Supreme Court ruled 5–4 in Obergefell v. Hodges in favor of same-sex marriage in all fifty states. The ruling invalidated limitations and bans on same-sex marriage throughout the country. As I write these words, it's too soon to know all the consequences of this decision.

However, the parliament of Great Britain passed its Marriage (Same Sex Couples) Act in 2013, legalizing same-sex marriage throughout England and Wales. With Britain's two-year head start, we can see what may lie ahead for America because of the overturn of the biblical and traditional definition of marriage. The so-called "marriage equality" law in Great Britain has been the camel's nose inside the tent for all sorts of rules and laws that now oppress people who hold traditional values.

Impact on language. Governing bodies ranging from Transport for London (London's mass transit authority) to major universities have adopted policies that prohibit "heteronormative" words such as *ladies* and *gentlemen*, or even gender-specific pronouns. Students at one university in northeastern England have been warned they will be marked down for using pronouns, such as *he*, that are not gender inclusive.[9] The suppression of traditional language is a way of controlling thought. If the secular leftists can tell you what words you can and cannot use, they can control the way you think. To see where this leads, read George Orwell's *Nineteen Eighty-Four*.

Impact on religious freedom. When Parliament debated same-sex marriage, politicians promised that safeguards would be built into the law to protect freedom of religion. No Christian would ever be required to violate his or her convictions. It took very little time for those promises to be broken.

In a July 2017 television interview, Minister for Women and Equalities Justine Greening said, "It is important that the church, in a way, keeps up and is part of a modern country. I wouldn't prescribe to them how they should deal with that but I do think we're living in a country where people broadly recognize that attitudes are in a different place now to where they were many, many years ago. We have allowed same-sex marriage, that's a massive step forward for the better. And for me, I think people do want to see our major faiths keep up with modern attitudes."[10]

A week earlier, John Bercow, Speaker of the House of Commons, said that gays and lesbians should be able to "bloody well get married in a church" if they want to.[11] And the church should have no choice but to comply.

Impact on religious expression. Some militant lesbian-gay-transgender advocates take it upon themselves to punish Christians who hold the "wrong" view on gender issues. Tim Farron once led England's third-largest political party, the Liberal Democrats. When journalists learned he was a practicing Christian, however, interviewers badgered him to explain his views on homosexuality. Did he believe what the Bible says about homosexuality? Did he believe that homosexual sex is sin? Farron had voted *in favor* of same-sex marriage in Parliament, feeling he should vote the views of his constituents instead of his own views. But that wasn't good enough for leftists.

Farron was hounded out of office for no other reason than

being a Christian. Upon his resignation, he said, "I seem to be the subject of suspicion because of what I believe. . . . We are kidding ourselves if we think we yet live in a tolerant, liberal society. . . . To be a political leader—especially of a progressive, liberal party in 2017—and to live as a committed Christian, to hold faithfully to the Bible's teaching, has felt impossible for me."[12]

Impact on children. Throughout the United Kingdom, children are subjected to "sex education" designed to promote positive attitudes toward homosexuality and transgenderism and to provide explicit instruction about many types of sexual activity. Even private religious schools are required to teach children these views. One private school, the Vishnitz Girls School in north London (an Orthodox Jewish school), faces closure purely because it does not give pupils "a full understanding of fundamental British values" regarding homosexuality."[13]

Impact on foster parenting and adoption. Great Britain is in the throes of a foster care crisis: too many foster kids, not enough foster parents. But the High Court of Great Britain has determined that kids are better off without parents than with Christian foster parents who teach the values of the Bible. A Christian couple, Eunice and Owen Johns, have been ruled unfit foster parents because of their religious convictions.

"All we wanted was to offer a loving home to a child in need," Eunice Johns said, "but because we are Christians with mainstream Christian views on sexual ethics, we are apparently unsuitable. . . . All we were not willing to do was to tell a small child that the practice of homosexuality was a good thing. We feel excluded and that there is no place for us in society." The Johns' attorney, Andrea Minichiello Williams, said, "The law has been increasingly interpreted by judges in a way which favours homosexual rights over freedom of conscience. Britain is now leading Europe in intolerance to religious belief."[14]

Impact on free speech. Ashers Bakery, a family-owned shop in Belfast, Northern Ireland, was found guilty of discrimination. The owners, an evangelical Christian couple, were ordered to pay £500 to a local gay activist for refusing to decorate a cake with Sesame Street characters Bert and Ernie and the slogan "Support Gay Marriage."[15]

Britain's National Trust, a volunteer organization devoted to nature conservation, ordered the 350 volunteers at the historic Felbrigg Hall to wear a "rainbow badge." Anyone not wearing the badge would be "moved out of sight" until they were willing to display the symbol of forced "tolerance."[16]

Britain's Marriage (Same Sex Couples) Act of 2013 was just the camel's nose. But once the nose is inside the tent, look out! Same-sex marriage is not merely about tolerance for gays. It's about intolerance against Christians. It doesn't stop with permitting same-sex couples to marry. Freedom of religion, conscience, and speech are all threatened. In 2015, the Supreme Court permitted this same camel to poke its nose into the American tent, and we can be sure that the rest of the ugly brute isn't far behind.

And this is certainly not the last time Christians will be marginalized. We can expect more strong-arm tactics from the left in the future. Yet no matter how those in power abuse our rights and try to silence us, we need to pray for our leaders and love them with the love of Jesus. We cannot be silent when they abuse their power and their office, but we must never act abusively in return. Jesus said we are to give to Caesar what belongs to Caesar, and give to God what belongs to God (Matthew 22:21).

Don't budge from the truth. Stand firm on God's principles

and God's law—but always be gracious and kind. Speak the truth in love.

Whether you call them liberals, progressives, or leftists, these folks believe in two things—their own enlightenment and the benevolence of the almighty State. They believe that, if only they could wield the power of the State to control our thoughts, speech, and behavior, they could impose their well-intentioned utopia on us all.

With his amazing power of foresight, C. S. Lewis seemed to understand today's utopian leftists decades before they arrived on the scene. He wrote, "Of all tyrannies, a tyranny sincerely exercised for the good of its victims may be the most oppressive. It may be better to live under robber barons than under omnipotent moral busybodies. The robber baron's cruelty may sometimes sleep, his cupidity may at some point be satiated; but those who torment us for our own good will torment us without end for they do so with the approval of their own conscience."[17]

JESUS AND SECULARISM

Tobias Jones, the bestselling author of *The Dark Heart of Italy*, warns of "an aspiring totalitarianism" of "would-be dictators" like Richard Dawkins and his fellow militant secularists. "Call them secular fundamentalists," Jones writes. "[They] are anti-God, and what they really want is the eradication of religion, and all believers, from the face of the earth."[18]

Extreme secularists, Jones says, make a show of tolerating religion as long as people keep their religion to themselves and never mention it in public. He observes that the secularists had great success with a deceptive tactic in which they "fostered the falsehood that wearing a crucifix or a veil or a turban was deeply offensive to other faiths. They pretended to be protecting religious sensibilities as a pretext to strip us of all religious expressions." The secularists convinced the State to ban religious symbols—and got what they wanted all along, an across-the-board ban on religious expression.[19]

Jones quotes secularist columnist Mary Riddell of *The Daily Telegraph*, who wrote, "Secularists do not wish to harm religion or deny its great cultural influence. They simply want it to know its place." In other words, Jones explains, Riddell is saying that religion should get in the closet and stay there.

Then Jones makes a fascinating statement—a statement that at first sounds shocking, but is absolutely true: "Jesus invented secularism." In Matthew 22:19-21, Jesus says:

"Show me the coin used for paying the tax." They brought him a denarius, and he asked them, "Whose image is this? And whose inscription?"

"Caesar's," they replied.

Then he said to them, "So give back to Caesar what is Caesar's, and to God what is God's."

Jesus was saying that there is a secular realm and there is a sacred realm. Prior to that moment, the realm of government and the realm of religion were intertwined. The best-known ancient kingdoms—from God's chosen nation, Israel, to the pagan kingdoms of Babylonia, Persia, Egypt, and Rome—were theocratic states in which kings were advised by, and accountable to, the priesthood. But Jesus said, in effect, that government operated within a public space in which the authority of government should be respected—but that authority could also be challenged if it ran afoul of God's law.

The old theocratic states were all-powerful and could not be challenged because the scepter of the king represented both civil and religious authority. But Jesus laid the foundation for the kind of government that is described in the American Constitution— a government that is secular in nature but founded on biblical principles, and that allows every citizen to worship in accordance with his or her own religious convictions.

There is nothing wrong with acknowledging that the realm of government is a secular realm—the realm of Caesar, as Jesus put it. After all, state churches often lose their vitality and restrict religious freedom. But when secularism itself becomes a religion, it turns oppressive and totalitarian. It spins out of control and becomes intolerant of Christianity and all other forms of religion. It ceases to be accountable to the people. It refuses to tolerate dissent by the people. It becomes an oppressor.

That is where today's secular fundamentalism is leading us. That is why we must confront secular fundamentalism, here and now.

The battle is already raging. You and your family are in the enemy's crosshairs. You cannot stand on the sidelines like a disinterested bystander. Everything you care about, everyone you hold dear, is at risk. It's time to step up and fight. In the remaining pages, we will discover how to fight that battle—and win.

FINDING THE TRUTH IN A POST-TRUTH WORLD

IN OCTOBER 2009, I preached at a huge tent meeting in the center of Alexandria, Egypt. It was an unprecedented evangelistic outreach, and seventeen buses brought people from all over the city. Many people made decisions to follow Christ or to recommit their lives to Him. The Westerners on our ministry team were amazed to see such a response to the gospel in Egypt's second-largest city.

At the same time, I sensed a troubling undercurrent, a mood of unrest that I hadn't felt during previous trips to Egypt. One change I noticed was that the Muslim Brotherhood—long banned as an illegal organization—now operated openly, holding demonstrations and making demands. Four months before my arrival in Egypt, President Obama had delivered an historic speech called "A New Beginning" at Cairo University. He had given legitimacy to the Muslim Brotherhood by insisting that at least ten members of the Brotherhood be in the audience for his speech.[1] President Obama's recognition of the organization had clearly emboldened them.

My hosts in Alexandria told me that when Christian university students distributed leaflets advertising my evangelistic meetings, Islamists went to the police and demanded the invitation be designated "For Christians Only." They didn't want Muslims to be evangelized. The police acquiesced to the Islamists' demands. Conditions were changing in Egypt—and not all for the good.

I was thinking of my 2009 experience in Alexandria as I watched the news on January 25, 2011. All across Egypt, a revolution had begun. It had started peacefully with demonstrations, occupations, marches, and strikes. Protesters, mostly young people, had demanded the resignation of Egyptian president Hosni Mubarak.

Soon, however, violent clashes broke out in which hundreds died and thousands were injured. Vandals torched police stations in Cairo, Alexandria, and other cities. Cairo's great circular plaza, Tahrir Square, became ground zero for a national protest movement, as uncounted numbers of people crowded together to demand a new government.

I was not surprised to see massive demonstrations at Tahrir Square—a place whose name means "liberation." It's a symbol of the people's yearning for freedom. But I was surprised to see the police and the army standing by and allowing the protests to go on. The army had maintained a firm and often brutal order in Egypt for nearly fifty years, but on this occasion, the army stood quietly, watching and waiting.

Tahrir Square was familiar to me. I had walked there many times in my youth and had preached many times at Kasr El Dobara Evangelical Church, just one block from the square. I knew many congregants at the church, including my nephew, who is an associate there. I talked with them by phone, so I had a direct line on events at Tahrir Square. The information I received from Egyptian Christians in Cairo was often at odds with the reporting on TV.

In the midst of these events, I received a call from a producer at CNN, inviting me to appear in the studio with CNN anchor Don Lemon to share my knowledge about what was happening in Egypt and Tahrir Square.

I agreed to be at the Atlanta studio on Saturday, January 29, from 5 to 8 p.m., thinking that Mr. Lemon wanted to hear my perspective as someone who was born in Egypt, who knew the Egyptian people and Egyptian society, and who was in daily contact with friends and family at the center of the crisis.

Early in our discussion,[2] I told Mr. Lemon that I had talked with family members in Cairo who had described looting at shops and banks. Young men stood guard on the sidewalks, brandishing clubs to protect their families and businesses from thugs and gangs.

"But this [uprising] is led largely by the youth," Lemon said, suggesting that the events in Cairo were nothing but a spontaneous protest by idealistic, freedom-loving youth.

I said, "It depends on who is using the youth."

"Why do you say that? Using the youth? Do you believe someone may be using them as a front?"

"Oh, no question," I responded. I acknowledged people's frustration with the Mubarak government over inflation, unemployment, and political repression. Many protesters sincerely wanted more freedom and opportunity. But others, I cautioned, were standing behind the scenes, watching the protests play out, ready to take advantage of the situation and seize power. I explained that some groups, including the Muslim Brotherhood, were upset with Mubarak because he had shut them out of the election and permitted women to be elected to parliament. They wanted to use this uprising to their political advantage.

Mr. Lemon, however, insisted that the Egyptians were

demanding full democracy now—and why shouldn't they get it? With all the poverty in Egypt, why shouldn't they be allowed to try something different?

I compared Egypt's situation to Iran in 1978 and '79, when freedom-loving young people had demonstrated in the streets, forcing the shah into exile. Once the shah was out, Ayatollah Khomeini had co-opted the revolution. Then he jailed or executed all the secular, Western-educated people who started the revolution, and the new Islamist regime was even more oppressive and totalitarian than that of the shah.

"But that is a worst-case scenario," Lemon said. "That doesn't mean that these people should not be protesting for what they believe is a democracy and a fair election process." Despite the looting and rioting in prisons, he insisted that most Egyptians didn't want to tear down their country but protect it.

I told Mr. Lemon I had no doubt that there were both Egyptian Christians and Muslims who wanted to see democratic change. Yet Egypt had no experience with a Western-style democracy, whose underpinnings had been written into the United States' founding documents. Meanwhile, I argued that President Mubarak, while far from perfect, seemed to be trying to make a gradual transition from the repressive Nasser- and Sadat-style Egypt to a more free and democratic Egypt. He was walking a tightrope, maintaining stability while trying to give the people more freedom, a little at a time. I wasn't defending the excesses of Mubarak's regime, but despite his faults, I thought he was trying to move the nation in a positive direction. Under his leadership, many people had moved from poverty into the middle class. And he had permitted opposition parties to operate freely and publish newspapers—something that never happened under Sadat. I worried that Egypt's next government would be more repressive than the government being tossed out.

Throughout our discussion, however, Mr. Lemon seemed determined to portray the uprising as one big happy experiment in democracy. The people were rising up to toss out the scoundrel, and the poor would be miraculously lifted out of poverty. The fact that history offered no precedent for this analysis didn't seem to trouble him at all. I suspect he simply wanted me to confirm his biases. In the end, those three hours turned into the most frustrating experience I'd ever had in broadcast media. I left feeling more discouraged than ever.

UNREST AND UPRISING

Mr. Mubarak had been president of Egypt since 1981, when his predecessor, Anwar Sadat, was assassinated. He had maintained the Camp David peace accords, which were forged between Egypt and Israel during the Carter administration. Though Mubarak had been a strong ally of the United States, the Tahrir Square protests convinced the Obama administration that Mubarak had to go. Observers around the world found the Obama administration's position baffling. *Israel Today* reported,

> White House spokesman Robert Gibbs legitimized future
> control of Egypt by radical Islamists when he said the
> next government in Cairo will have to include "important
> non-secular actors." . . . The only significant non-secular
> actor on the Egyptian stage is the Muslim Brotherhood, . . .
> [which] is the forerunner of groups like Hamas and the
> Islamic Jihad, and counts among its former members

Ayman al-Zawahiri, Al Qaeda's second in command. . . . The Muslim Brotherhood lists as one of its goals the total subjugation of the entire world to Islam and the establishment of an Islamic empire.[3]

Once an Islamist government seemed inevitable, the Obama administration made a calculated decision to support the Muslim Brotherhood in its attempt to gain control of Egypt. Apparently, the administration hoped the organization would be grateful for American support, and this would give the United States an opening with the new Islamist government in Egypt.

The Egyptian uprising lasted until February 11, when Mr. Mubarak resigned and transferred power to the armed forces. An Islamist, Mohamed Morsi, ran for president. A longtime leader of the Muslim Brotherhood, Morsi had been arrested along with other leaders of the group on January 28, 2011, and he escaped from Cairo's Wadi el-Natroun prison during a massive jailbreak two days later. Egypt held two elections in May and June 2012. The Muslim Brotherhood candidate, Mohamed Morsi, won a plurality in the first round and a slim majority in the second.

President Obama and the American media didn't seem to understand the tactics the Muslim Brotherhood used to subvert the election. The Islamists were far less popular in Egypt than they appeared to be. To magnify their influence, the Muslim Brotherhood placed thugs at many polling places to intimidate Christian and moderate Muslim voters. Voter turnout in both elections was surprisingly low, about 46 percent in the first round, 52 percent in the second, which suggests that voting in Egypt was suppressed.

The warnings I had shared on CNN quickly came to pass.

The Muslim Brotherhood had been patiently working to achieve power since its founding in 1928, and the 2011 uprising gave them the opening they had been waiting for. Once Mohamed Morsi came to power, the Brotherhood could finally Islamize the country. In the process of imposing hard-line Islamist rule, the Morsi government brought the nation to its knees. The business climate declined, jobs dried up, and poverty deepened. Fear and distrust spread throughout the strictly regimented society.

Why would President Obama withdraw his support from Mr. Mubarak, a longtime ally, in favor of a leader of the Muslim Brotherhood? He said he was respecting the will of the Egyptian people. Once Morsi had been elected, the US president said he would support the new government in Egypt as it made the "transition to democracy." But I believe another part of the answer may lie in some of the advisers President Obama had gathered around him. A few examples:

Dalia Mogahed, one of the president's advisers on Muslim affairs, was a controversial figure even before President Obama appointed her to the White House Office of Faith-Based and Neighborhood Partnerships. She once appeared on a British television show hosted by Ibtihal Bsis of the extreme Islamist group Hizb ut Tahrir (which seeks to create a one-world Islamic caliphate with global Sharia law). During her appearance on the show, Mogahed said, "The majority of women around the world associate gender justice, or justice for women, with sharia compliance."[4]

Another adviser, Mohamed Elibiary, served on the Homeland Security Advisory Council from 2010 to 2014. He frequently told people he was a conservative Republican, though as a teenager he had been mentored by Hamas leader Shukri Abu Baker. He also had supported the Hamas-backed Holy Land Foundation until it was shut down by the US government for terrorism-related activities. Furthermore, Elibiary was an outspoken defender of Sayyid Qutb, an early Muslim Brotherhood leader.

Elibiary has sent numerous pro-Islamist messages from his Twitter account. In October 2013, while serving the Obama White House, Elibiary wrote, "I do consider the United States of America an Islamic country with an Islamically compliant constitution." The following year, as ISIS was overrunning Iraq and Syria, he tweeted, "Kind of comical watching pundits on some US TV channels freak out about an #ISIS #Caliphate." Later that year, he tweeted that the establishment of an Islamic caliphate was "inevitable." He was forced to resign from the Homeland Security Advisory Council in September 2014 under pressure from Congress.[5]

With advisers such as Mogahed and Elibiary, it's small wonder that US foreign policy tilted in favor of Muslim extremists.

After Morsi won the election, President Obama phoned him and congratulated him on his victory. And much of the media in Europe and America fell right in line. They announced the story with headlines like, "The First Democratically Elected President in Egyptian History." To the uninformed, the Egyptian election results sounded like good news.

But for those of us who knew what to expect from the Muslim Brotherhood, this outcome was anything but good. As I expected, the newly elected Morsi wasted little time in issuing a decree that placed him above the law—and effectively made himself dictator of Egypt. Yet from the White House, we heard only muted criticism. A Morsi victory was the result the Obama administration had hoped and worked for. President Obama and Secretary Clinton couldn't afford to admit that their own foreign policy had helped install an anti-Western, Islamist radical as the dictator of Egypt.

Twelve months of Morsi's dictatorial rule brought Egypt to its knees—economically, socially, and politically. I share the view of many Egyptians who believe that Morsi did more harm and stirred up more opposition in a single year than Mubarak generated in three decades. Yet the story went mostly unreported by the major newspapers and networks. Why? Because it didn't fit the narrative.

The Obama administration had determined that an Islamist leader would be good for Egypt and good for the Middle East, and the reporting of its media allies reflected this perspective. Blinded by their ideology and their desire to be thought of as "enlightened" in the Muslim world, the White House and the mainstream media covered up the deteriorating situation in Egypt.

Finally, on June 30, 2013—exactly one year to the day after Morsi was sworn in as president—the people of Egypt rose up. According to Shady Ghazali Harb of Egypt's National Salvation Front political coalition, an estimated 30 million people from all walks of life and religious persuasions shouted as one, demanding new elections.[6] Millions joined mass demonstrations that erupted across the country. Once again, protesters jammed Cairo's Tahrir Square. Islamist dictators don't like having their authority questioned, and they detest re-elections. Morsi threatened the protesters with a crackdown. But when Morsi summoned the army to move in and quell the demonstrations, he was stunned to learn that the army stood by the protesters. A military coalition, headed by Egyptian army chief Abdel Fattah al-Sisi, gave Morsi an ultimatum: Resolve your differences with the demonstrators or face removal from office.

President Obama responded with a statement that he was "deeply concerned" over the actions of the Egyptian military, and he urged the military leaders to return the nation to "democratically elected" rule.[7] He seemed unaware that the Egyptian people themselves were fighting for democracy. That's why they had taken to the streets. It appears that, to President Obama, democracy meant keeping Morsi in charge. While it's true that Morsi had been elected, the Obama administration did not seem at all concerned that, once in office, Morsi had taken a sharply authoritarian turn.

Also, during Morsi's time in office, the mainstream media ignored another big story: God's intervention in Egypt. The twelve months of the Islamist dictatorship of Mohamed Morsi were marked by the open persecution of Egypt's Christian minority, which numbers about 10 million people. Despite the threats and attacks by Islamist gangs, Christians packed out church services and prayer meetings. Some prayer meetings were held around the clock, so that there was never a time when hundreds or thousands of Egyptian Christians weren't crying out to God for justice and protection. When Morsi refused to meet the demands of the military coalition, the military removed him from office and al-Sisi, the defense minister, took charge. Though he was unelected, I believe al-Sisi has been a good leader, having taken such positive steps as reestablishing religious tolerance and treating both Christians and Muslims fairly.

With the ouster of Morsi, the newly outlawed Muslim Brotherhood sought vengeance against the most convenient targets: Christians. They burned Christian churches, homes, and businesses. Yet the Christians viewed these acts of retribution as a small price to pay for a better future for their country. Many Egyptians—including many nonbelievers—concluded that the fall of the Muslim Brotherhood–led government was a direct answer to the prayers of Egyptian Christians. But try explaining that to the BBC, NBC, ABC, CBS, or CNN.

Here's an even *bigger* story that the media largely ignored—and this was *good news*: In January 2014, during the Christmas and New Year celebrations in Egypt, interim president Adly Mansour—a practicing Muslim—visited the Coptic Christian cathedral in Cairo. There he met and shook hands with the Coptic patriarch, Tawadros II, and expressed the good wishes of all Egyptians for Christmas and the New Year. In 1,400 years of majority-Islamic rule in Egypt, that had never happened before. It was a meeting of historic significance, not only for Egypt and the region, but for all tolerant and moderate Muslims. The Islamist government of Mohamed Morsi and the Muslim Brotherhood had produced only violence, repression, and distrust. The meeting between President Mansour and the Coptic patriarch demonstrated that national unity and stability could be achieved if the rights of everyone, including religious minorities, were respected.

But the journalistic mind-set favors a narrative of conflict and division. If there are images of angry protests or bloody street battles, both print and broadcast outlets will leap into action with frightening headlines. As the journalistic saying goes, "If it bleeds, it leads." But if the story is about a historic gesture of goodwill between Muslims and Christians, an event that could alter and positively impact the future—well, the networks and newspapers simply aren't interested.

Egyptian Christians persevered through the upheaval and persecution by Mohamed Morsi's regime, demonstrating to believers here in the West that making a Christlike stand for the truth—no matter the cost—can achieve miracles. Speaking the truth in love shouts more loudly to the world than any newspaper, television show, or social media platform can.

FILTERING REALITY

In February 2017, the *Washington Post* changed its slogan from "The Paper That Digs Deeper" to "Democracy Dies in Darkness." I agree that democracy requires sunlight to thrive. That's why the founding fathers wisely gave us the First Amendment to the Constitution, which guarantees not only free speech and freedom of religion, but freedom of the press. In order for people to prudently govern themselves through a democratically elected representative government, they need to know the truth.

Publishers and broadcasters certainly have a constitutional right to publish falsehoods and mislead their readers. It's unethical for a news outlet to lie, but it's not unconstitutional, and it happens all the time. Sometimes the media does so by blindly following a party line; at other times, they bury important stories because they miss their significance. Wise consumers of the news need to be aware of how reliable and truthful their news sources are—and should not support news outlets that suppress the truth.

News reporters, editors, and broadcasters are human beings, and all human beings have their biases. To be biased doesn't necessarily mean to be dishonest. A bias is often nothing more than the filter through which we see reality. For instance, I recognize that my frustration over the media's coverage of recent events in Egypt is due in part to my heritage and desire to see freedom take root there. Our biases are shaped by our experiences, by the people we talk to, and by the information we take in. Part of the problem with human bias is that we are usually not even aware of it.

Take, for example, the story of Mansour's visit to the cathedral. It's possible that people in newsrooms across the country saw the wire story of Egypt's interim president's Christmas visit and simply did not recognize it as news. It didn't bleed, so it didn't lead. There was no conflict, there were no guns firing, and there were no bodies in the streets, so it wasn't news. It may well be that the people making journalistic decisions that day simply lacked the historical awareness to recognize the significance of that event.

But that's not a valid excuse. A journalist's job is to sift through the events of the day, find those that are significant, and report the truth, fairly and squarely. All too often, the news that is printed and broadcast seems to be cherry-picked to sell papers or to manipulate public opinion in a predetermined—and biased—way.

We all need to be aware of our biases and of how those biases prevent us from recognizing the truth. We all tend to live in ideological bubbles. Once we have formed a worldview—Christian, Muslim, atheist; conservative, liberal, centrist—we tend to filter all of reality through that worldview. We accumulate evidence for the view we hold, and we screen out information that contradicts it.

We hang out with people who think like us, talk like us, and value the same things we do. We watch news channels and read books, magazines, and websites that reinforce our beliefs. If a friend posts something to Facebook that we disagree with, we may "unfriend" that person. We recall stories and events in a way that confirms our beliefs. The tendency to take in only information that confirms our worldview is called confirmation bias.

No one is immune to confirmation bias. Atheists are guilty of it—but so are Christians. Liberals get caught up in it—and so do conservatives. One of the strangest cases of confirmation bias ever reported was a conspiracy theory that went viral during the 2016 presidential election. That conspiracy theory was known as Pizzagate.

In July 2016, the WikiLeaks website began to publish a collection of e-mails stolen from the Democratic National Committee. In November, a trove of e-mails from Hillary Clinton's campaign chairman John Podesta were posted there. Conspiracy theorists on the far right began poring over these e-mails, sometimes jumping to bizarre conclusions. When someone found the phrase "cheese pizza," for instance, he concluded that these were code words for "child pornography." After all, both phrases have the initials C. P.

As these theories were bouncing back and forth in the nether regions of the Internet, the stories became embellished with additional details, including lurid accounts of satanic rituals. Eventually, the narrative emerged that Mr. Podesta and Mrs. Clinton were involved in a vast child sex-trafficking ring that operated out of a pizza parlor in Washington, DC. The story quickly spread through social media. The stories even included photos of the restaurant's interior, many of which turned out to be fake. Even though law enforcement agencies try to knock down wild rumors like these, the stories and speculations took on a life of their own.

For some people, it simply wasn't enough to disagree with Mrs. Clinton's politics, her failure to act in the Benghazi tragedy, or her reckless decision to keep State Department e-mails on a private server in her home. They had to accuse her, without any evidence, of the most horrible crimes imaginable, which involved satanic rites and unspeakable crimes against children.

The owner and employees of the pizza parlor received harassing phone calls and death threats. Other businesses on the same block were hounded and threatened for not doing anything about the supposed "child sex ring" down the street. Even pizza parlors in other parts of the country were badgered, as if it were somehow a crime to sell pizza.

Finally, in December 2016, a man from North Carolina drove to Washington, DC, walked into the pizza shop, and fired three shots from an AR-15-style rifle. Though no one was injured, the customers and workers thought they were about to die. The man proceeded to search the pizza parlor, looking for evidence that the conspiracy theories were true. He found none, and later admitted, "The intel on this wasn't 100 percent."[8] That was a serious understatement.

I will tell you right now that I'm no fan of Hillary Clinton. But I am a devotee of the truth. We do no credit to our beliefs by clinging to lies, bizarre speculation, and baseless conspiracy theories. There's a natural human tendency to dismiss any news that doesn't fit our own biases and narrative as "fake news." It's a natural human tendency to swallow whole whatever we *want* to be true and to push away whatever we *don't* want to be true. We are all susceptible to *confirmation bias*, the tendency to uncritically accept whatever conforms to our beliefs and preconceived notions—and the tendency to reject information that contradicts our preconceptions.

But we have a responsibility to the truth. We have a responsibility to be skeptical even when certain stories seem to support our worldview. We have a responsibility to check out quotations we find on the Internet to make sure that Mark Twain or George Washington or Shakespeare really said them. (As Abraham Lincoln once said, "You can't believe everything you read on the Internet.")

One of my favorite stories that illustrates how confirmation bias can keep us from recognizing the truth is about Pauline Kael, the longtime film critic for the *New Yorker*. When President Nixon defeated Senator George McGovern in 1972 in one of the biggest landslides in American political history, an astonished Ms. Kael supposedly said, "I can't believe Nixon won! I don't know anyone who voted for him."

The only problem with that story is that it never happened. Ms. Kael did once remark in a speech that she knew only one person who voted for Nixon—but she wasn't claiming to be surprised by the election results. Yet the story has been told and retold so many times as evidence of liberals' privileged provincialism that it has taken on a life of its own.

If we are going to be people who stand for the truth, we need to learn to sort truth from falsehood. We need to stop lies in their tracks—including the falsehoods that come from our own side.

UNINFORMED OR MISINFORMED?

In a world of media bias, fake news, and Internet rumors, when we are so prone to confirmation bias and our own unconscious filtering of reality, how can we know what's true and what's false? How can we know the truth in a post-truth world?

Mark Twain is widely quoted as saying, "If you don't read the newspaper, you are uninformed. If you do read the newspaper, you are misinformed." Now, this statement is another example of fake quotes on the Internet. There is no proof that this statement originated with Mark Twain, even though it is attributed to him on numerous websites and in books of quotations.

Even though Mark Twain probably never said it, there's a lot of truth in that quotation. If you never read a newspaper or watch TV news, then you probably don't know what's going on in the world. But if you consume a lot of news, odds are you are going to be misinformed. You are going to "know" a lot of things that just aren't so.

We don't want to be uninformed. And we don't want to be

misinformed. We want to have informed opinions when we talk to our friends and neighbors, when we write letters to our elected representatives, and when we go into the voting booth to cast our sacred ballot. How, then, can we know the truth? How can we learn to detect when our news sources are biased or are offering incomplete or untrue information?

The situation isn't hopeless. There are ways to make sure you are not taken in by biased reporting, fake news, and Internet rumors. Here are some suggestions:

1. *Don't automatically believe early reports.* When a news story—whether a terror attack, a workplace shooting, or a political scandal—is breaking, you can pretty much count on one thing: Many details in the early reports will be wrong. As you listen to the reporter, suspend your judgment and wait for more complete facts to emerge.

2. *Don't believe information from anonymous sources.* When a reporter says that his or her source refused to be identified, there is a good chance the information is untrue. If the reporter quotes a named source or puts someone on the air to tell his or her story, there's a much better chance the story is true. People who leak stories anonymously almost always have a hidden motive. Don't let them manipulate your thoughts and feelings. Be skeptical of stories from unnamed sources.

3. *Don't believe stories that simply cite other news outlets.* A false or biased news story doesn't become true by being repeated by other media sources.

4. *Watch and read multiple news outlets, and compare their coverage.* If you get your news from just one news source, there's a good chance you are getting a skewed impression of world events. Avoid taking in news only from outlets that confirm your biases. Try to find media with a good track record of getting their facts right.

5. *Pay attention to the language and tone of your news sources.* Do your media outlets seem to be trying to whip up your emotions? Do they make certain facts or events sound more sinister than they really are? Do you sense that your news sources are trying to manipulate you and shape your opinions?

6. *Be sure your news sources correct their mistakes promptly and fully.* Reporters and news organizations make mistakes. That's part of being human. But when their stories are exposed as false or erroneous, many news outlets don't bother to apologize or correct the error. A newspaper or news broadcast that admits and corrects its errors is more trustworthy than one that doesn't.

7. *Don't let the news media manipulate your emotions, your behavior, or your outlook on life.* The broadcast, print, and Internet news purveyors have figured out that one key to holding an audience is to generate anger. All a news anchor has to say is, "Coming up next, a story that will make your blood boil"—and you're likely to stay tuned through a cavalcade of commercials. Visit a news website and notice all the headlines designed to make you mad. Rage generates

clicks, and clicks generate revenue. One reason our nation is so angry and divided is that outrage is good for the news business. Don't let the rage profiteers manipulate you.

Don't be uninformed. Don't be misinformed. Be a smart and skeptical news consumer so you can be an informed and responsible citizen.

GRACE AND TRUTH AND THE AMERICAN MEDIA

In addition to following the guidelines above, remember that the media is made up of people and organizations with their own biases and worldviews that affect their reporting. In January 2013, the Obama White House announced that prominent evangelical pastor Louie Giglio would give the benediction at President Obama's second inauguration. Afterward, operatives of a far-left organization, the Center for American Progress Action Fund, went to Pastor Giglio's website and downloaded audio files of all his messages—and discovered one entitled "In Search of a Standard—Christian Response to Homosexuality."

In that message Pastor Giglio accurately referred to homosexual activity as "sin in the eyes of God, and . . . in the Word of God." He also warned that the gay rights movement sought to make homosexuality "accepted as a norm in our society."

Reaction from the gay rights community was swift. Wayne Besen, founder of the ironically named Truth Wins Out, said, "It is imperative that Giglio clarify his remarks and explain whether he has evolved on gay rights, like so many other faith and political leaders. It would be a shame to select a preacher with backward views on L.G.B.T. people at a moment when the nation is rapidly moving forward on our issues."[9]

On January 10, the *New York Times* reported that the voices of protest from the gay activist community had caused the White House to rethink its selection of Louie Giglio. The online *Times* story contained a paragraph that read,

> An official with Mr. Obama's Presidential Inaugural Committee said the committee, which operates separately from the White House, vetted Mr. Giglio. People familiar with internal discussions between administration and committee officials said the White House viewed the selection as a problem for Mr. Obama, and told the panel on Wednesday night to quickly fix it. By Thursday morning, Mr. Giglio said he had withdrawn.

In other words, the *Times* was implying that the Obama White House had disinvited Pastor Giglio. That was embarrassing for President Obama, because it would offend Christians to know that Pastor Giglio was dropped *precisely because* he preached the biblical perspective on human sexuality. The Obama camp correctly perceived that Christians would see the White House action for what it was: an assault on religious liberty.

So a few hours after the news story appeared on the *New York Times* website, it was replaced by another version of the article. The new version was the same as the original version *except* that the entire paragraph I quote above had simply disappeared.[10] Now, that is a violation of journalistic ethics. It's a violation of the *New York Times'* editorial policy. The *Times'* own policy is that it must correct its errors, and each correction must be noted at the bottom of the page. This policy dates to an earlier era, when the *Times* sought to be "transparent" and honest about its mistakes.

The journalist who noticed the removal of that paragraph contacted the *New York Times* reporter who wrote the story. The *Times* reporter claimed she removed it after a White House spokesperson contacted her to say it wasn't true. But if that's so, why didn't the *Times* issue a correction rather than simply scrub the information off its website as if it had never existed? There's a term for attempting to make information disappear from a webpage without a trace. It's called memory-holing.

It's possible that the *New York Times* memory-holed the Pastor Giglio paragraph on its own, without any pressure from the Obama White House. That seems unlikely since it was done in violation of the *Times'* own policy. Regardless of their reasoning, the *Times* helped the Obama White House hide the embarrassing fact that the president had discriminated against an evangelical pastor for preaching God's uncompromised Word.[11]

But there's an even more important issue involved here. Clearly, the Obama administration and the *New York Times* came to the same conclusion: There was something wrong with inviting a minister of the gospel who preached the uncompromised Word of God to participate in the inauguration.

Why did the gay activist community demand that Pastor Giglio be disinvited? And why did the Obama White House surrender to that demand? It's because gay rights activists have been successful in flipping the moral scales upside down. We live in a post-truth age in which there are no moral absolutes, so the gay rights coalition has been able to position its agenda as the "moral high ground." They say, "All gay people want to do is to love each other. Whether it's heterosexual or homosexual, love is love. Are you against love? Why are you so hateful?"

They have managed to identify biblical morality and God's commandments with "hate," while identifying immorality and practices the Bible forbids with love. With the help of their allies on the political left, the religious left, and the media, gay activists have successfully smeared Bible-believing Christians as bigots and haters.

It's interesting that when Barack Obama was running for president in 2008, his position on same-sex marriage was exactly the same as mine is today. He said, "I believe marriage is between a man and a woman. I am not in favor of gay marriage." But during his first term in office, public opinion polls began to tilt in favor of same-sex marriage—and Mr. Obama's opinion began to "evolve." In an interview with ABC News on May 9, 2012, he said, "I've been going through an evolution on this issue. . . . I've just concluded that for me personally, it is important for me to go ahead and affirm that I think same-sex couples should be able to get married."[12]

Now, I have not "evolved" at all on this issue—and I don't expect to. The authority of God's Word does not permit me to evolve my opinions on matters that God has settled with finality. The left will label me a hater and an extremist for holding firm to the principles of God's Word—and while I don't enjoy being misjudged for remaining faithful to the Bible, that is simply one facet of the persecution that Jesus Himself told us to expect as His followers.

It's important to understand that the activists and propagandists don't represent all people with same-sex attraction. There are many people who struggle with their sexual identity, many who live celibate lives in spite of their homosexual tendencies, and many who do not engage in the gay pride movement with all of its political activism and flamboyant parades.

Believing in God's Word does not make me—or you—a hater. It does not make us bigots or homophobes. I have always reached out as a pastor and a believer to befriend those who are in the homosexual lifestyle. I don't hate them—I love them with the love of Jesus Christ. For example, I have gay neighbors in the high-rise building where I have offices. Whenever I pass them in the hall or share an elevator with them, I greet them and shake their hands. "How are you?" I genuinely want to know, but they generally freeze up and barely acknowledge me. They know that I'm a Christian pastor, and to this day, they are very standoffish. But I'm going to continue caring for them.

When I talk to homosexual people, I don't treat them differently than I would treat anyone else. I don't soft-pedal what the Bible says about their lifestyle, but I also don't rub it in or tell them that they are morally inferior to me or anyone else. They are sinners in need of grace, and I am a sinner saved by grace. That is the truth, straight from God's Word. That means that when I am talking to any person caught in a lifestyle of sin, regardless of what that sin may be, I have an obligation to extend to that person the grace and truth of Jesus. We are to treat fellow sinners the same way Jesus treated the woman caught in adultery. In John 8, the enemies of Jesus brought the woman to Him and demanded to know if she should be stoned, as the Old Testament law required. He answered, "Let any one of you who is without sin be the first to throw a stone at her" (verse 7). Her accusers all departed, one by one. No one remained to condemn her. And in verse 11 Jesus told her, "Neither do I condemn you" (that's grace). But He also added, "Go now and leave your life of sin" (that's truth).

This word *grace* is widely misunderstood in our culture. In the Bible, grace simply refers to God's gifts of goodness and blessing in our lives that we do not deserve—gifts of salvation, eternal life, forgiveness of sin, mercy, protection, material blessings, family, and so forth. All of these things come from the grace of God.

That is why I first approach others with news about the saving grace of Jesus Christ. I share with them the good news that God loves them and sent His Son to die for them as an atonement for sin. Sinners need grace, but they also need truth. The world loves grace—but hates truth. The world wants us to embrace and affirm not only the sinner, but the sin as well. Today the world even says we must take what God forbids and turn it into a sacrament—the unholy "sacrament" of same-sex marriage. But I love God, I love His Word, and I love people too much to compromise God's truth.

As Christians, we must never diminish God's grace, and we must never compromise God's truth. Whatever sins you may have committed, I do not hate you for them. I will not condemn you for them. But I will tell you the truth about your sins from God's Word.

Here is the truth—the absolute truth—that you will probably never read in any newspaper or hear on any news broadcast: A genuine Christian who follows the example of the Lord, who speaks God's uncompromised truth, and who shares the good news of God's lavish grace is the *best friend a sinner could have*. A genuine Christian is the best friend a drug addict or alcoholic could have, the best friend a workaholic or liar could have, the best friend an adulterer or fornicator could have, and, yes, the best friend a homosexual man or woman could have.

If you are a Christian, I appeal to you in the name of Jesus to be an example of Christ to the people around you. Be an example of grace and truth to everyone you meet, no matter their sin, no matter how they mock you or hate you, no matter how they revile His name. Pray for them. Love them. Be the grace of Christ and the truth of Christ in their lives, and someday they may come to love the Lord Jesus too.

NOBLE SEEKERS OF TRUTH

The Bible is filled with admonitions and principles about truth. From Genesis to Revelation, God's Word warns us not to be ignorant, but to seek the truth. Certainly, the most important truth we are to pursue is the truth contained in God's Word. Yet God does not want us to be ignorant or misled in *any* area of truth. His Word contains valuable insights into how we are to approach any truth claims.

We see this principle in a scene from Acts 17. Paul was on his second missionary journey when he met stiff opposition in the city of Thessalonica. Many of the Jews there rose up in anger because he preached that Jesus is the Messiah who was prophesied in the Old Testament. The angry crowd rioted and chased Paul out of the city. The people of Thessalonica had been deceived by their biases. Many refused to listen to the gospel because it didn't agree with what they already believed. Paul had come to give them the Good News, but they thought that the gospel was "fake news."

So Paul and his friend Silas moved on to another town, Berea, and there Paul again preached the good news of Jesus Christ. Acts 17:11-12 tells us, "Now the Berean Jews were of more noble character than those in Thessalonica, for they received the message with great eagerness and examined the Scriptures every day to see if what Paul said was true. As a result, many of them believed, as did also a number of prominent Greek women and many Greek men."

Why were the Bereans of "more noble character" than the people of Thessalonica? It's because they were willing to set aside their biases and preconceptions, and they were willing to listen to Paul's news. Now, they weren't gullible. They weren't going to take Paul's word at face value. The Bereans were open-minded but skeptical. They were willing to listen, but they fact-checked every claim Paul made to see if what he said was true.

People who seek the truth are noble in God's eyes. The search for truth is an important quest. The Berean people didn't merely want to have their biases confirmed. They were willing to set aside their biases and prejudices—but only if Paul's message was backed up by evidence from Scripture.

And that's exactly how God wants you and me to pursue the truth, whether we are studying God's Word or the world around us. That's why, in 1 John 4:1, the apostle John writes, "Dear friends, do not believe every spirit, but test the spirits to see whether they are from God, because many false prophets have gone out into the world." In other words, if someone comes to you with a message that is supposedly from God, put that message to the test. Compare it to God's Word.

If you are listening to a Christian teacher or preacher, examine the Scriptures to see if what that person says is true. In fact, I urge you to test everything I say in this book against God's Word. Don't just take my word for it. Make sure that everything I say is in accordance with Scripture. Be open-minded, but be skeptical. Verify the message, that it is a godly and biblical message, and be a noble student of the Bible. As Paul told Timothy, "Do your best to present yourself to God as one approved, a worker who does not need to be ashamed and who correctly handles the word of truth" (2 Timothy 2:15).

As believers, this is perhaps most important within our places of worship. These days, many new teachings and false gospels are worming their way into the church. If we are not noble students of God's Word, we risk being taken in by false teachers and fake news. Even in the church, all too many people today have ceased to believe in absolute truth. They say such foolish things as "You have your truth, I have my truth, and who's to say what is right or wrong?" They have confused truth with opinion.

We all have opinions, but we don't all have the truth. Opinions change, but truth is eternal. There are many opinions, but there is only one truth—and God's great desire is that we all come to a saving knowledge of His Truth. As Paul wrote, "This is good, and pleases God our Savior, who wants all people to be saved and to come to a knowledge of the truth" (1 Timothy 2:3-4).

Jesus often spoke of the truth—and in John 14:6, He told us that He Himself is the Way, the Truth, and the Life. One of the most quoted statements of the Lord Jesus is John 8:32: "Then you will know the truth, and the truth will set you free." In fact, you might be surprised to learn that Allen Dulles, the fifth director of the Central Intelligence Agency, had that verse carved into the marble wall of the original CIA headquarters building. Dulles was the son of a Presbyterian minister, and he wanted a biblical statement about truth to remind everyone who entered CIA headquarters that the agency's mission was to search for truth. That verse, quoted from the King James Bible, reads, "And ye shall know the truth, and the truth shall make you free," and it is the CIA's unofficial motto to this day.

But it's important to remember that the full meaning of that verse can be understood only by reading the verse that precedes it. The entire passage, John 8:31-32, reads, "To the Jews who had believed him, Jesus said, 'If you hold to my teaching, you are really my disciples. Then you will know the truth, and the truth will set you free.'" The Lord's teachings are truth, and only His teachings will set us free. When quoting the Lord's promise that the truth will set us free, we should always quote those two verses together.

And what are the consequences of turning aside from God's truth? The prophet Isaiah explains:

Woe to those who call evil good
    and good evil,
who put darkness for light
    and light for darkness,
who put bitter for sweet,
    and sweet for bitter
Woe to those who are wise in their own eyes
    and clever in their own sight.

ISAIAH 5:20-21

Such spiritual blindness can lead to troubling consequences, including the belief that everyone is entitled to their own "truth"— even when it contradicts obvious reality.

In his book *Truth: A Bigger View of God's Word*, Randy Alcorn tells the story of a man who visited several American universities to conduct research. He wanted to know if college students still believed in seeking the truth. What he learned was shocking. This researcher was a white male in his midthirties, standing about five foot nine. He interviewed groups of students and asked them a series of questions.

"What would you think if I told you I am a woman?"

The students thought that was just fine. If he wanted to identify as a woman, why shouldn't he?

"What if I told you that I'm Chinese?"

Though he was clearly as Caucasian as could be, the students all said that whatever he wanted to call himself, however he wanted to identify himself, was fine.

"And what if I told you that I'm seven years old?"

The students had to think about that for a moment. They admitted that he certainly didn't appear to be seven years old. But after a few moments of reflection, they decided that if he wanted to identify as a seven-year-old, why not? In fact, several said they would have no problem if he wanted to enroll in elementary school as a seven-year-old.

Finally, the researcher said, "What if I told you I'm six feet five inches tall?"

Again, some of the students struggled with this question—but ultimately, they came to a consensus that if this five-foot-nine man wanted to identify as six-foot-five, who were they to judge him?

The students had been taught that the most important values are tolerance and acceptance of everyone's right to identify themselves in any way they wish. They had not been taught to value the truth.

Those students are the future of our society. They are the future of Western civilization. It would be fair to say they are the future of the church.

Randy Alcorn concludes with a stunning statement by American philosopher Allan Bloom from his book *The Closing of the American Mind*: "There is one thing a professor can be absolutely certain of: almost every student entering the university believes, or says he believes, that truth is relative."[13] Bloom wrote these words more than thirty years ago, and they are even more relevant today.

Truth is not relative. Truth is absolute. It is real, even if no human being on earth is willing to recognize and acknowledge it. You and I must learn to seek the truth, verify the truth with evidence, accept the truth, and preach the truth at every opportunity.

Followers of Christ are, first and foremost, followers of truth.

WILL POLITICAL ISLAM DESTROY WESTERN CIVILIZATION?

AT ALMOST 10 P.M. on Saturday, June 3, 2017, in the Southwark district of London, a white van rumbled onto London Bridge. The van bounced up onto the walkway and accelerated quickly, plowing through helpless pedestrians at high speed. It crashed outside a pub on Borough High Street.

Three men piled out of the van, armed with foot-long knives. They proceeded to hack and stab people in their path, as well as in the pubs and restaurants along the street. Realizing they were under attack, the bystanders fought back, throwing bottles or chairs at the knife-wielding men. Witnesses later said that the attackers shouted, "This is for Allah!"

The horrifying melee lasted about ten minutes before armed officers of the London police arrived. Officers fired fifty rounds in about twenty seconds, killing all three of the knife-wielding men.

No one was surprised when Home Secretary Amber Rudd declared the attackers to be Islamist terrorists. Soon after that, the Islamist news agency Amaq announced that the Islamic State of Iraq and Syria (ISIS) claimed responsibility for the attack.

In all, eight innocent people were killed and forty-eight were injured. It was the third deadly terrorist attack in the United Kingdom in four months, following attacks in Westminster in March and Manchester in May.

The next morning, Prime Minister Theresa May delivered a speech on Downing Street, calling for a stepped-up effort to confront extremism and prevent terrorism in Great Britain—and she offered a four-point plan to achieve that goal:

First, *confront the Islamist ideology*. Islamist extremism, she said, "will only be defeated when we turn people's minds away from this violence and make them understand that our values—pluralistic British values—are superior to anything offered by the preachers and supporters of hate."

Second, *stop giving the Islamist ideology a safe place to breed*. This means policing the Internet so that the terrorists can no longer use cyberspace as a place to hide and plot their murderous acts.

Third, *stamp out Islamic extremism across society*. May said, "There is—to be frank—far too much tolerance of extremism in our country. So we need to become far more robust in identifying it and stamping it out across the public sector and across society. That will require some difficult, and often embarrassing, conversations. But the whole of our country needs to come together to take on this extremism."

Fourth, *review and update the nation's counter-terrorism strategy*. "It is time," May concluded, "to say 'Enough is enough.'"[1]

TWENTY YEARS TOO LATE

In response to Prime Minister May's speech, I penned "An Open Letter to the Leaders of Great Britain," which was posted at *The*

Daily Caller and *Fox News*. I praised Prime Minister May's remarks and the stronger antiterrorism measures she promised—but I pointed out that her speech came two decades too late:

> *For more than twenty years, the British government and the British media have acquiesced to the demands of Islamists. As a result, the Islamists have grown more and more confident that they have instilled enough fear to get whatever they demand.*

The Islamist demands included the power to prevent a Dutch political leader (an outspoken anti-Islamist) from entering Great Britain; the power to target and harass non-Muslims in East London with impunity; the power to create about eighty-five Sharia councils in Great Britain that sanction horrifying "honor beatings" of Muslim women on British soil.

I concluded my appeal this way:

> *As a Bible-believing Christian, the only hope I see is if the Christian leaders in England would call for a day of fasting and prayer. By humbling themselves before God, they can seek His mercy—and seek the boldness to act on the course outlined in Prime Minister Theresa May's speech.*
>
> *If they don't act now, it may be too late.*

For decades, our Western culture has been only vaguely aware of the Muslim world. If you look at the entertainment media of the twentieth century, you'll see that Western movies and TV largely treated Arabs and Muslim extremists as more of a joke than a threat. From old black-and-white comedies like *Road to*

Morocco and *A Night in Casablanca* to films of the 1980s such as *Airplane!*, *Back to the Future*, and *Raiders of the Lost Ark*, American motion pictures have generally portrayed Muslims dismissively or even derisively—but have rarely taken Middle Eastern culture seriously. For decades, the Muslim world has seemed remote and irrelevant to our daily lives.

Then came 9/11, and everything changed.

For the first time, many people began to consider the origin of the Muslim faith. The Islamic religion was founded in the seventh century by Muhammad. From its beginning, Islam's goal has always been the establishment of a world empire. It expanded rapidly under Umar ibn al-Khattab, the second caliph to succeed Muhammad. Umar conquered most of the Byzantine Empire and all of Persia within a few years. While Christianity has spread by evangelistic appeal, Islam has expanded by the sword (as my Muslim teachers in Egypt taught me).

In the past, Muslim armies conquered much of modern Spain, swept across central France, and poured into Germany and Austria. The armies of Islam conquered cities that had once cradled the early Christian church, including Antioch, Damascus, and Jerusalem. They obliterated the once-vital church of North Africa.

This is all ancient history, some say—yet the political and military struggles of recent decades have their roots in the waves of Islamic invasions that took place centuries ago. To this day, radical Islamists refer to the people of Western civilization as "Crusaders," and what we call "ancient history" the Islamists consider "current events."

In January 2014, the *New Yorker* published an interview with President Obama, who dismissed Islamic terror groups like ISIS as the equivalent of a junior varsity basketball team trying to compete in the NBA. Within two years, the "junior varsity" terror group ISIS had conquered a vast region in Iraq and Syria, dominated more than eight million people, and launched or inspired deadly attacks in Europe and America.

The Syrian Observatory for Human Rights estimates that there have been as many as one hundred thousand ISIS fighters in Iraq and Syria. As of February 2017, the United States–led coalition in Iraq believed that a two-year military campaign against ISIS had killed more than sixty thousand Islamic State militants. The Pentagon estimated in 2016 that there are about fifteen thousand ISIS fighters remaining in Iraq and Syria.[2] Even so, ISIS continues to sponsor deadly attacks, such as the brutal 2017 attacks in England.

More troubling is the news that Al Qaeda—the parent organization of ISIS—is experiencing a resurgence. According to the International Crisis Group, Al Qaeda has reconstituted its strength and its numbers in the Arabian Peninsula and is now much stronger and more dangerous than it ever was while its founder, Osama bin Laden, was alive.[3] In fact, one of Al Qaeda's current leaders is bin Laden's son, Hamza, who is bent on revenge for the killing of his father. He has stated, "I consider myself to be forged in steel. The path of jihad for the sake of [Allah] is what we live."[4]

Equally disturbing, Colin P. Clarke, a political scientist with the RAND Corporation, reports that another terror group that splintered from Al Qaeda—Jabhat Fateh al Sham (JFS, formerly known as Jabhat al Nusra)—"may pose a more significant long-term threat to the West than the Islamic State in Iraq and Syria (ISIS). . . . With approximately 10,000 fighters, JFS is now both the largest al Qaeda franchise and by many accounts, the most lethal. . . . [The failed state of] Syria is the ideal staging ground for al Qaeda to rejuvenate its global campaign of terrorism through JFS."[5]

"I THANK GOD FOR ISIS"

Let's be clear: Islamists—extreme radical Muslims seeking to conquer the world by the sword—are a minority in the Muslim world. Growing up in Egypt, I had Muslim school friends even though I came from a Christian family. To this day, I have many fine friends who are moderate Muslims. These Muslim friends label adherents of political Islam as Islamists. They are as appalled by Islamism as we are.

One underreported trend of recent years is the growing number of Muslims who are investigating the claims of Jesus Christ. Moderate Muslims appear to be the most open to the gospel of Jesus Christ. They are willing to sit down and exchange views with Christians in a rational and cordial way. Many of them are embarrassed by the violence and cruelty displayed by ISIS and other Islamic terror groups. They believe that the actions of these extremists are a disgrace to their faith and to Allah.

Even though the number of Christian converts in the Muslim world remains small, this phenomenon has caught the attention of Muslim hard-liners, and they are angered by it. In fact, I believe the fear of fellow Muslims turning to Christ has caused the terrorists of ISIS and other Islamist groups to ratchet up the violence they inflict on fellow Muslims.

Yet even while the horror of ISIS has shocked the world, I heard of one young Saudi woman who *thanked God* for ISIS. Can you imagine being thankful for ISIS? Yet this young woman, only eighteen years old, was thankful because the atrocities of ISIS had opened her eyes to the emptiness and hopelessness of Islam.

For her protection, I'll call her Samar. She lives in Mecca, the holiest city of the Islamic religion. Throughout her childhood, she was steeped in the teachings of the Qur'an. Once she reached her teen years, however, she began to question what she had been taught. Samar became even more disturbed as she heard about the atrocities inflicted on the world by Al Qaeda, ISIS, and other Islamist terror groups. How could these Muslim extremists take joy in the slaughter of children—including Muslim children? And how could Allah be pleased by so much torture and slaughter in his name?

So this young woman began seeking the truth. She investigated Christianity by watching THE KINGDOM SAT, the twenty-four-hour satellite channel of Leading The Way, which beams Christian programming into the Arab world. Though she had many questions about the Christian faith, she was drawn to the God of love depicted in the Bible.

Samar's parents suspected she was watching Christian TV, so they blocked the Christian channel from their satellite receiver. But Samar would not be turned away from her quest for the truth. She contacted the follow-up team of THE KINGDOM SAT and told the phone counselor that she could be killed if her family found out she was investigating Christianity. "I want to know for sure that Jesus is the Truth, as He said," she told the counselor. "I'm not ready to die for a lie."

Over an eight-month period, Samar continued to call the follow-up team with questions about Jesus. By the end of that time, she was firmly convinced that Jesus was not merely a prophet, as the Qur'an claimed. She knew He was the living Son of God and the Redeemer of the world—and she prayed to receive Jesus as her Lord and Savior.

"Now I am ready to die," she told the counselor, "because it's easy to die for the truth."

The phone counselor said that Samar's courageous statement as a new believer moved him to tears. Samar also made another profound statement the night she prayed to receive Christ: "I thank God for ISIS for opening my eyes."

Samar is the only person I've ever heard of who is sincerely grateful to God for ISIS. But I understand why she feels that way. If ISIS had not demonstrated to her the moral and spiritual emptiness of Islam, she might never have gone on a quest for the truth of Jesus Christ. In fact, through our global ministry, Leading The Way, we hear from many Muslims around the world who are disillusioned with Islam, often because of the atrocities committed by terrorists in the name of Allah.

Today, Samar shares her faith in Christ with her friends who are doubting and questioning Islam. At the risk of her life, this courageous young Christian is God's ambassador in Mecca, the fortress of Islam.

In recent years, I have received many reports of Muslims who are turning to Christ. The reign of terror of ISIS in Syria and Iraq sent thousands of refugees fleeing from their homes—and many of them opened their hearts to the gospel. You won't read their stories in your morning newspaper or see them being interviewed on the evening news, but I can tell you that God is at work in the Muslim world, and many people are turning from the crescent of Islam and clinging to the cross of Christ.

We easily forget that extremists and terrorists do not represent all Muslims. I believe the majority of Muslims are moderate and reform-minded. They are embarrassed by the horrors committed by terrorists in the name of their religion. They don't want to be lumped together with these extremists, and they want the terrorists to be described as what they truly are—not just "Muslims," but

"Muslim fundamentalists." Make no mistake, a Muslim fundamentalist is still a Muslim, and when a Muslim fundamentalist uses the sword to behead an "infidel," he is following the foundation of his faith. But not all Muslims interpret the Qur'an the same way.

I deeply admire two Muslim heads of state, Jordan's king Abdullah and Egyptian president Abdel Fattah al-Sisi, for courageously and steadfastly opposing radical political Islam. King Abdullah is a constitutional monarch who has maintained Jordan as an island of economic and political stability surrounded by a turbulent sea of Islamic hostility and unrest. Because Jordan remains prosperous and stable, it was one of the few Muslim-majority nations that was not rocked by the Arab Spring uprisings of 2011. Abdullah is popular with his people, respected internationally, and trusted widely for promoting dialogue and understanding between Muslims, Christians, and Jews. He is the official guardian of the Muslim and Christian holy sites in Jerusalem.

Egypt's president, al-Sisi, has openly professed his goal of modernizing Islam and has issued a call for a "revolution" within Islam to reform the faith and cleanse Islam of the extremism, intolerance, and violence that drives groups like ISIS and Al Qaeda. In a speech before Muslim clerics, he called on them to interpret the Islamic texts in an "enlightened" way. Radical fundamentalist interpretations of the Qur'an, he added, were "making enemies of the whole world." Al-Sisi has even attended Christmas services at Coptic Christian churches, and he has declared that the people of his nation "should not view each other as Christians or Muslims, but as Egyptians."[6]

I admire and affirm Abdel al-Sisi for his courageous commitment to stand for the truth during dangerous times. Of course, I hope and pray that he will come to know the One who is the

Way, the Truth, and the Life—but I admire him for openly proclaiming the truth that Islam has a problem with the sword and bloodshed. Al-Sisi has risked his life to challenge the imams to seek a new and reformed interpretation of the Qur'an that is appropriate for the times in which we live. I support reforms that would bring an end to terror and needless bloodshed.

As a Christian, I love the Muslim people. I am commanded to love and not to hate. I long for Muslims to come to the one true God and to the Messiah who died on the cross to save sinners. Thousands of Muslims are already coming to know Christ as their Savior. There is room for many more. Every human heart has a desperate need to know God, even though some do not recognize that need.

A COUNTERFEIT "GOSPEL"

Despite my hope that disillusioned Muslims like Samar and moderate Muslim leaders like Egypt's al-Sisi will help reform their religion, radical Islamists still pose a grave danger. The Islamist invasion of Western civilization has begun. Does this mean that ISIS and other Islamist terror groups will conquer the West? Will radical political Islam defeat America and Britain? Will Islamists conquer and destroy the Christian church?

I'm convinced that you and I are the only ones who can determine the answers to those questions. After investing decades studying and researching the root causes of the Islamist resurgence and the decline of Western civilization, I have concluded that America, Great Britain, the West, and the church cannot be conquered from without unless they are first hollowed out and destroyed from within.

The great tragedy of our time is that Western civilization is already well on its way toward collapse and destruction from within. Unless we repent and change direction as a culture, *our own foolishness* will destroy our civilization—and the Islamists will simply walk in and take over. Our children and grandchildren will pay the price of our folly and sin.

Abraham Lincoln is often quoted as saying, "America will never be destroyed from the outside. If we falter and lose our freedoms, it will be because we destroyed ourselves." That is a paraphrase of a statement from Lincoln's Lyceum Address, delivered more than two decades before he became president:

> Shall we expect some transatlantic military giant to step the ocean and crush us at a blow? Never! All the armies of Europe, Asia, and Africa combined . . . could not by force take a drink from the Ohio or make a track on the Blue Ridge in a trial of a thousand years. . . . If destruction be our lot, we must ourselves be its author and finisher. As a nation of free men, we must live through all time or die by suicide.[7]

Will America die by suicide? History appears to be moving in that direction—but the story of America does not have to end that way.

I don't fear the Islamic jihadists nearly as much as I fear the Christian church in the West departing from the Scriptures. Militant Islam has always grown when Christianity became weak. And militant Islam has always retreated when Christianity was strong. When is Christianity strongest? When it remains true to God's Word.

In its early history, Islam grew like a parasite on the corpse of the Christian church—a church that had become riddled with heresies and apostasy. Immediately before the rise of Islam, false gospels spread across the Middle East and up into Europe and down into Arabia. Centuries before the Internet was invented, Satan was spreading false "memes" that quickly "went viral" throughout the ancient world. These false gospels presented a polluted image of Christ. They distorted the truth of our faith beyond all recognition. The Arabian Peninsula was especially open to falsehood and resistant to the pure truth of the gospel—for two reasons:

First, the Arab people practiced a form of idolatry that was a mixture of pagan and Hebrew ideas. The tenets of Judaism were familiar to the early Arabian people, and pre-Islamic worship at the Kaaba (the granite cube-shaped structure in Mecca) was based in part on Jewish patriarchal traditions. Though Christianity is the fulfillment of Judaism, the polluted forms of Judaism observed in the Arab peninsula tended to harden people's hearts against the truth of the gospel.

Second, the "Christianity" practiced among the Arab people in the seventh century was largely corrupted by Gnostic heresies and arguments over the nature of Christ. Some of these pseudo-Christian cults taught the false, unbiblical doctrine that Jesus was a mere human being who achieved divinity through mystical knowledge. The pagan pre-Islamic Arabs rejected this weak pseudo-Christianity. When true Christian missionaries came to them with the authentic gospel, the Arabs said, "We've already heard about your Christ and want nothing to do with Him." Yet they remained spiritually hungry, searching for a religious rebirth. They were ripe for a bold message of religious transformation.

Satan was preparing a man to bring the Arab people a counterfeit gospel, a false messenger of a counterfeit religion. In AD 610, this man emerged from a cave on Mount Hira near Mecca. His name was Muhammad Ibn Abd Allah, from the Hashemite clan of the Quraysh tribe. He had just received a vision, and he went forth with a new set of "revelations."

Perhaps if the authentic gospel of salvation by grace through faith in the Lord Jesus Christ had reached Muhammad's ears, he might have been a great saint, a great evangelist, an Arabian apostle Paul. Instead, Muhammad founded a religion that has become the fiercest opponent Christendom has ever seen.

Before the rise of Islam, Christianity had become the dominant faith across the Middle East, North Africa, and Europe. But alongside the true "wheat" of the Christian church, "weeds" of false doctrine and false faith had sprung up. These religions pretended to be Christianity, but they were actually breakaway cults with such names as Arianism (which taught that Christ was a subordinate being, neither co-equal nor co-eternal with God the Father), Nestorianism (which split the deity of Christ from the humanity of Christ), Sabellianism (which denied the Trinity), and Ebionism (which claimed that Jesus is the Messiah but not God, and which demanded legalistic observance of Jewish law).

Muhammad was strongly influenced by the Ebionite heresy, which he mistakenly thought of as orthodox Christianity. Muhammad had an Ebionite cousin who taught him the Old and New Testaments, though his teachings were tainted by Ebionite doctrines. After the death of his cousin, Muhammad was left on his own to try to understand God's truth. The tragic result was a new religion—the cult known as Islam.

Muhammad's view of Christianity was largely shaped by false believers and their heresies, but the early church was not always riddled with falsehood and heresy. The North African church had once been powerful and influential, the home of such revered church fathers as Cyprian of Carthage and Augustine of Hippo. But by the fifth century, the once-strong North African church had been infiltrated by false teachers. There were thousands of churches across the region, but many of them had lost their biblical moorings and had fallen away from the faith.

From 647 to 648, Muslim armies under Caliph Umar marched across Egypt and into what we now know as Libya. Many Christians were so biblically uninformed that they actually welcomed Islamic teachings into the church as a kind of new revelation. As a result, many so-called Christians allowed their churches to be turned into mosques without putting up a fight.

A second wave of Islamic conquest swept North Africa from 665 to 689, taking control of the region from the nominally Christian Byzantine Empire. A third wave of conquest, from the early 690s to 709, enabled the Islamic caliphate to take complete control of North Africa. Most scholars believe that the church in North Africa effectively ceased to exist at that point. Christian boys were "converted" to Islam at swordpoint, forced to renounce Jesus, and made to fight as soldiers in Muslim armies.

Although the heresies of Muhammad's time are no longer common, Western Christianity is being weakened by new heresies and factions, including:

Universalism: The belief that everyone will be saved or that all religious paths lead to God and eternal life.

Progressive reconstructionism: An interfaith movement focused on environmental and progressive issues as a means to achieve world peace, universal disarmament, and social justice.

The emerging or postevangelical church: A movement that tries to make the gospel more palatable to a postmodern culture by taking an inclusive approach to various belief systems, emphasizing emotions over absolute truth, and rejecting the existence of hell, judgment, or the need for forgiveness.

Insider movement: A group of people who claim to follow Jesus while remaining within the religious community of their birth, such as Islam or Hinduism.

Hypergrace: The overreaction to legalism, resulting in abuse of God's grace as believers seek freedom, not just from legalism, but also from God's standards.

Chrislam: The attempt to merge Christianity and Islam.

The truth about Jesus—that He is God incarnate, the sacrifice for our sin, the only begotten Son of the Father, full of grace and truth—is the heart of Christianity. If you take the heart out of the body, you are left with a corpse with "Christian" stamped on its forehead. That's the belief system Muhammad saw in his world, and it's no wonder that Islam, the false religion he founded, is now the sworn enemy of the Christian faith.

The goal of Islam has not changed since the time of Muhammad. Islamists are still intent on finishing the work of Muslim conquest. Today they seek to subjugate the Christian West through a three-pronged strategy: (1) a program of intimidation—everything from accusing opponents of being "Islamophobic" to threats of violence and terrorism; (2) migration and an Islamic baby boom; and

(3) the use of Arab oil wealth as a way of influencing or controlling Western governments and institutions.

The Islamist strategy is working. France and Germany each have nearly 5 million Muslims living within their borders.[8] And in Great Britain, the Muslim population is growing at a rate ten times faster than the population as a whole, according to a 2009 report in the *Times* of London, which said, "The Muslim population in Britain has grown by more than 500,000 to 2.4 million in just four years, according to official research collated for *The Times*. . . . In the same period the number of Christians in the country fell by more than 2 million." The increase, the *Times* added, "was attributable to immigration, a higher birthrate, and conversions to Islam."[9]

In the name of tolerance, many European countries seem to have welcomed the influence of Muslims they consider middle-of-the-road. For a time, that included Sheikh Yusuf al-Qaradawi, chairman of the International Union of Muslim Scholars, who was regarded by the mainstream media as a "moderate" Muslim spokes-man. As a result, he was often interviewed or invited to speak to groups of Westerners who wanted to hear a Muslim view of world events. For example, in 2004 al-Qaradawi was invited to address a London conference called "Our Children, Our Future," sponsored by the London Metropolitan Police and Britain's Department for Work and Pensions.

Yet this same "moderate" Muslim sheikh said, "We will conquer Europe, we will conquer America!" Al-Qaradawi also justifies suicide bombing as a legitimate form of Islamic jihad. "It is not suicide," he said. "It is martyrdom in the name of God. I consider this type of martyrdom operation as an indication of the justice of Allah almighty. Allah is just. Through his infinite wisdom, he has given the weak what the strong do not possess and that is the ability to turn their bodies into bombs as the Palestinians do."[10] He also said, "Israelis might have nuclear bombs, but we have the children bomb and these human bombs must continue until liberation."[11]

Concern over his views finally spread, and by 2012, al-Qaradawi had been banned from entering Great Britain and France. (He'd been prohibited from entering the United States in 1999.) Still, Sheikh al-Qaradawi's strategy is well on its way to being accomplished. How, then, should we in the West respond? Unfortunately, some of our leaders and pundits seem oblivious to the threat.

BARTERING AWAY OUR FREEDOM

Critically important events are happening today—and you are not hearing about them. These events will impact your life and the lives of your children and grandchildren—yet they are being ignored or kept hidden from you and the rest of the American people. One of these events is a series of international conferences called the Istanbul Process. The stated purpose of these conferences is to help Afghanistan and neighboring countries discuss ways to cooperate in fighting terrorism, extremism, and poverty. But there is more to the Istanbul Process than meets the eye.

The Istanbul Process was named after the site of the first conference in Turkey, which was held in November 2011. The United States and other Western nations help with funding, but the agenda of the Istanbul Process is driven by the Organization of Islamic Cooperation (OIC), consisting of all fifty-seven of the world's Muslim countries. French journalist and political commentator Alexandre del Valle warns that the goals of the OIC—and the hidden agenda of the Istanbul Process—are twofold: (1) to impose Sharia law on all countries and populations in the Muslim world; and (2) to Islamize the West, primarily through Muslim immigrants who refuse to assimilate and integrate themselves into Western society.[12]

The Istanbul Process holds a conference every year, and the goal seems to be to keep moving the ball of Islamization and Sharia law further and further down the field, yard by yard, inch by inch, until the OIC can sneak the ball into the end zone. The organization uses a variety of issues to advance its agenda.

For example, the OIC created its own answer to the Universal Declaration of Human Rights that was adopted by the United Nations in Paris in 1948. Though the OIC's statement also includes the term *human rights*, the Cairo Declaration of Human Rights in Islam is based on Sharia law, which allows honor killings, the treatment of women as property, an array of brutal punishments for various crimes, and so forth. Because the Cairo Declaration is based on Islamic law, it claims to be superior to the UN's 1948 document because, of course, Islamic law is superior to all non-Islamic law. Though the Islamic declaration has no binding effect, the UN has legitimized it—and the OIC has again moved the ball further down the field.

Another issue the OIC has exploited to promote the Islamization of the West is a concept called "defamation of religion." Alexandre del Valle explains:

> This concept is a serious threat to our democratic values because it aims at restricting freedom of speech as a way to "prevent intolerance" and religious hatred.

It strangely compares the right to criticize Islam—
a *religion*—to a *racist crime* and to ethnic hatred or
insult. . . . [Any criticism] against Islam is penalized and
targeted as "racist," even in Europe.[13]

Alexandre del Valle also points out that the term *Islamophobia*,
which we constantly hear in our own culture from the apolo-
gists for Islam and Islamism, was actually coined by the Ayatollah
Khomeini in 1990 as a justification for sentencing novelist Salman
Rushdie to death in absentia. Since then, the term has been used
widely by the American left to shame anyone who sounds an alarm
about radical Islamism in America. It's a way of silencing opponents by labeling them as haters and bigots. Clearly, the Ayatollah
Khomeini's scheme has worked brilliantly because the term he
coined for propaganda purposes has wormed its way into the
everyday language of the political left and the mainstream media.

Under the Obama administration, America cooperated closely
with the OIC and the Istanbul Process, helping to fund and promote the effort to Islamize America and the West. Our tax dollars
have been spent to undermine our constitutional freedoms. One
of the key instruments the OIC has used in its effort to Islamize
the West (with the enthusiastic assistance of the Obama administration and other Western governments) is UN Human Rights
Council Resolution 16/18, which was adopted by the Human
Rights Council in March 2011. The stated goal of Resolution
16/18 is to encourage tolerance and religious diversity around the
world. But the way it seeks to accomplish this goal is by banning
any speech that is critical of Islam (even if that criticism is 100 percent accurate), all in the name of "tolerance" and "diversity."

Stephen Coughlin, a senior fellow at the Center for Security

Policy, explained the ramifications of Resolution 16/18 for our American freedoms and way of life: "This is a direct extraterritorial demand that non-Muslim jurisdictions submit to Islamic law and implement shariah-based punishment over time. In other words, the OIC is set on making it an enforceable crime for non-Muslim people anywhere in the world—including the United States—to say anything about Islam that Islam does not permit."[14]

By supporting Resolution 16/18 and the Istanbul Process, America has given the Organization of Islamic Cooperation political legitimacy in its desire to silence any voice, including the voice of reasonable Muslim scholars, from criticizing Islam in any way. Our tax dollars have helped finance and further the Islamists' goal of imposing Sharia law on the American people and the American Constitution.

We in the West need to wake up to the fact that our political leaders have been systematically selling us out to political Islam. We need to be aware of and alert to what is going on around us. We can't afford to simply vote one political party out and another party in, and assume that the problem has been fixed. Whether there is a Republican or a Democrat in the White House, whether Congress leans left or right, we need to be involved, writing letters and e-mails to our elected leaders, posting on social media, talking to our friends and neighbors, and letting people know that our freedoms are being bartered away.

Why are so many of our politicians eager to cooperate with those who seek to Islamize America and the West? I'm convinced that the reason for the blindness of our politicians comes down to secular thinking. The word *secular* comes from the Latin word *saeculāris*, which means "worldly," or "pertaining to this present age." Our politicians tend to look at the world in secular terms—in terms of momentary political advantage, economic forces, and geopolitical power. They don't understand that the Islamists with whom they cooperate and negotiate are operating from a very different view of the world.

The Islamist mind is not a secular mind. Muslim extremists see themselves as surrounded by an invisible world—a world governed by Allah and his laws. One of these rules is that Muslims must conquer territory in Allah's name. Another is that unbelievers or infidels must surrender and submit to Islam and to Allah. Muslims also believe that if they die in the act of killing infidels, they will immediately enter paradise, where all their desires will be sated with alcohol, virgins, and sexual pleasures. This invisible world is real to the Islamist—every bit as real as the physical world around him.

I'm not saying that all Muslims embrace this worldview. I have many moderate Muslim friends and acquaintances who would reject it. But the leaders of most Islamic nations tend to be extremists who live in the invisible world of their radical religion—and when they negotiate with secular leaders of the West, they are quietly, cleverly advancing an Islamist agenda of gradual world conquest and the establishment of a global caliphate.

I have been writing and speaking about the Islamist agenda for decades, and my message has been greeted with skepticism and disbelief by people across the political spectrum. Now, unfortunately, the tragic events I predicted are coming to pass. Islamists keep making demands that come from otherworldly motivations inherent in Islamist thinking—and we keep trying to appease the Islamists with our secular-based accommodations. We compromise with the Islamists on such initiatives as the Istanbul Process and UN Human Rights Council Resolution 16/18—and we don't realize until it's too late that we ourselves have brought the Trojan horse into the walls of our fortress. We have cooperated in our own destruction.

If politicians in the West truly want to protect their fellow citizens and save their civilization, they must study the Islamist mind. This is the realization Prime Minister Theresa May arrived at after the London terror attack of June 2017. But as I noted in my open letter, that realization has come twenty years too late. The old secular thinking has been delusional—and suicidal. It's time for a new approach to the threat that Islamism poses to our civilization.

MY WISH FOR ALL MUSLIMS

When I was a Christian student in Egypt, I felt a deep burden to reach the Muslim community with the gospel. For a time in 1982, I even visited a group of Islamist Egyptians who called themselves "Jihad." This group was a forerunner of the organization now known as Al Qaeda. I observed that these young Islamists were intensely committed to their religion and their cause. I realized that if this movement continued to grow, it would become a threat to the entire world. They knew I was writing a PhD dissertation on them, and they made it clear that, for my own safety, I had to write only what they told me to write. Their intense zeal for the purity of Islam was a challenge to me: Was I as committed to loving others in the name of Christ as they were committed to conquering the world in the name of Allah?

The Qur'an contains many suras, or chapters, that speak of peace and generosity—and it contains many suras that are militant, warlike, and even cruel. The gentler passages of the Qur'an came from the earlier stages of Muhammad's life, when he saw himself as preaching the same message as Moses and Jesus. The more militant passages of the Qur'an came from the later stages of Muhammad's life, when he was involved in a protracted military campaign with the polytheists on the Arabian Peninsula.

Moderate Muslims tend to focus on the gentler passages. They view the militant and violent passages as applying to an earlier time. This doesn't mean that Muslims obey some parts of the Qur'an and reject others. It simply means that moderate Muslims emphasize some parts of the Qur'an while extreme Islamists prioritize the more confrontational and violent texts. But all Muslims believe that every revelation in the Qur'an was given to Muhammad by the archangel Gabriel in order to establish monotheism in Arabia.

The Islamists, and many on the left in America and Europe, will tell you that if you share the gospel of Christ and challenge Muslims' beliefs, then you are being unloving toward them. If you criticize Islamic beliefs or culture or law in any way, then you are an "Islamophobe," a person who irrationally fears and hates Muslims. Let's not be afraid of being called "Islamophobes" for speaking the truth. Let's not be cowed into silence by those who seek to conquer our civilization.

Instead, let's pray for boldness as we carry out the great commission of our resurrected Lord Jesus Christ: "All authority in heaven and on earth has been given to me. Therefore go and make disciples of all nations, baptizing them in the name of the Father and of the Son and of the Holy Spirit, and teaching them to obey everything I have commanded you. And surely I am with you always, to the very end of the age" (Matthew 28:18-20).

Our challenge as Bible-believing Christians is to present the good news of Jesus to the entire world, including the Muslim world, and to do so truthfully, lovingly, and fearlessly. We must never compromise God's truth that Jesus is the Way, the Truth, and the Life—and that He is the only way to God the Father.

God is doing an amazing work in the Middle East, and our international evangelistic organization Leading The Way is a part of that work. We are beaming Christian television programming into the Muslim world twenty-four hours a day, seven days a week, with the potential of reaching 160 million homes across the Muslim world that are equipped with satellite TV receivers.

Let me tell you about a man I'll call Hakeem (not his real name). He learned to read the Qur'an when he was just three and a half years old. His grandfather led worship at the local mosque. As a boy, Hakeem believed he would follow in his grandfather's footsteps. He was as committed to the Muslim religion as it is possible to be.

When he was eighteen, Hakeem accidentally tuned in to a Christian radio station that broadcast the gospel in Arabic. It captured his attention—and though he knew that as a good Muslim, he should not be listening, he had to hear more. After listening to the broadcast, he couldn't stop thinking about Jesus. Again and again, when he was alone in his room and was sure no one could overhear, he'd turn on his radio and listen to the Christian message.

Soon—almost against his will—he was praying to the God he had been hearing about on the radio. He called out, "God, if You are really there, show me a sign!"

Then, in what could only be an answer to the prayer he had just prayed, the radio announcer read the words of John 3:16— "For God so loved the world that he gave his one and only Son, that whoever believes in him shall not perish but have eternal life."

There was no doubt in his mind. Hakeem knew that this was

the sign he'd been seeking. Alone in his room, he went to his knees and prayed to receive Jesus.

A short time after his conversion, his parents learned that he'd become a Christian. His father beat him—then pulled a gun and fired at the young man. Hakeem ran for his life, knowing that he no longer had a family.

Hakeem had an unquenchable desire to share the good news of Jesus with Muslims—even though he knew he would face persecution and maybe even death. He eventually made contact with our Leading The Way team in his country. A few years ago, he left his home country and settled in North America.

Today Hakeem is the North American follow-up coordinator for Leading The Way. He understands the questions Muslims ask. When they call, seeking to know more about Christ, he is uniquely equipped to share God's truth with them and to lead them to Jesus. He also helps connect new believers to Arab-speaking churches.

How can we defend our civilization against the Islamists who seek to conquer us? How can we defend the church against the Islamist invaders? How can we know that it's not too late for America and for Western civilization? Certainly we need to speak the truth boldly, refusing to back down because of the threats of Islamists or the jeers from those on the left who tell us to be "tolerant." But more than that, we need to be as courageous and committed as Hakeem, who would not even let the rejection of his own family keep him from sharing the life-giving gospel he had found.

How can we share the good news of Jesus Christ with our Muslim friends and neighbors and with Muslims around the globe? God is preparing and opening the hearts of many Muslims, near and far. You may have thought that they were unreachable, but they're not. Many are disillusioned by the terror and violence that their religion has inspired around the world. Muslims are hungering for the truth as never before. (See pages 189–191 for ideas on how to talk with Muslims about your faith.)

We can pray for a revival in the church, and we can pray for a great wave of evangelism and conversions among the Muslim people. God loves them every bit as much as He loves you and me. We have what they need. We have God's truth. If we have the love of Christ living in us, we will boldly share that truth.

ILLUSION AND DELUSION—
OR TRUTH?

LYNN BARBER is an English journalist who writes for the *Sunday Times*. In May 2017, she published a personal—and anguished—story of her encounter with a young Muslim man. She described watching the daily horror stories of Syrian refugees who drowned at sea or suffocated in hot trucks while trying to escape the war in their homeland. Her heart was broken by the photo of a mother stranded with her baby in the sea after fleeing Syria, struggling to keep the child above the waves. "I decided I must do something," she wrote—not just signing a petition or sending an e-mail to her member of Parliament, but something meaningful.

A woman in her seventies, Lynn had a large home. Couldn't she take in an asylum seeker? She wrote to her local council, offering to host a refugee family, but learned she was ineligible because she smoked. Through a friend, however, she was introduced to a young Sudanese man named Mohammed. He was polite, spoke English, and had an ID card that made him an official asylum seeker. He received a weekly £35 welfare stipend from the British government while awaiting his asylum hearing. Lynn took Mohammed into her home, assuming he might have to wait several weeks for his hearing—but later learned it could be a matter of *years*.

Lynn trusted him with her front-door key, burglar alarm code, and access to her computer. Mohammed told her that he planned to treat her like his mother. She didn't care for the sound of that and told him to treat her as his landlady instead.

Over dinner one night, Mohammed told her the story of his journey toward asylum—getting into unspecified trouble while studying at Khartoum University and then being smuggled over the desert by truck into Libya. That was followed by a sea voyage to Italy, detention in an Italian jail, and a rail journey into France. For the final leg of his journey, he stowed away on a ferry boat that took him across the Channel to England. It was a harrowing tale, filled with obstacles and perils. Her heart went out to the young man as he told it.

When friends learned that Lynn had taken a young Muslim man into her home, they warned her that he could be dangerous. But she wasn't concerned even though there were problems that she tried to ignore. For instance, he broke the clothes dryer and never cleaned the washing machine. Once as the postman dropped mail through the slot in her front door, Lynn's housekeeper watched him walk over the letters instead of picking them up. One time, he asked Lynn where the nearest park was because he wanted to buy some dope. And it was odd that, though he supposedly lived on a mere £35 a week, he never lacked money.

Mohammed often asked Lynn to turn up the heat in her home. One warm autumn day, he asked again. She refused. He insisted, saying his feet were cold, and then adjusted the thermostat without her permission. Furious, she told him to put on extra socks. They argued—and later he apologized in a note he slipped under her door, which said, "Sorry and I feel shame too." This made her feel guilty. Maybe Mohammed didn't have any warm clothes. So she collected cast-off clothes from her friends to give to Mohammed.

Her friends told her she was a saint, taking in an asylum seeker. But she didn't feel altruistic. In fact, she confessed that her reasons for taking Mohammed into her home were somewhat selfish. "I was getting bored with my own comfort," she wrote, adding, "I needed a bit of a shake-up. . . . Giving a room to Mohammed seemed like a neat solution."

After Mohammed had lived with her about six months, she wrote a few pages about the experience of having him as her houseguest. Then she had Mohammed read what she had written. His reaction surprised her. He was upset—but wouldn't explain why. He avoided her for days, and finally she demanded that he explain what was wrong.

At first he would only moan and shake his head. Finally, he blurted, "I am not a refugee! I am a political leader! My family is very rich! We could buy you up like that. Do you want money? Is that why you write this filth? I get you money. You First World women are all the same, you are heartless. You have no feelings. You Christians are all racists." After a long, incoherent rant, he concluded, "I can no longer live in this house."

"No," Lynn said, "you can't."

She was frightened of Mohammed now—not because she thought he would physically attack her, but because she feared he had lost his mind. She let him get his belongings together and escorted him out of the house—but forgot to demand that he return the key to the front door. She lay awake all that night, worrying that he might come back and let himself into the house.

"I felt such a fool," she wrote. On the one hand, Mohammed had never stolen from her and had never deliberately harmed her. On the other hand, he had deceived her, and she was sure he had secretly hated her during the six months he had lived in her house.

After Mohammed left, she discovered hundreds of photos on her computer—photos of his journey from Africa to Europe and England, as well as photos of him and his friends sightseeing in France. Most of his supposedly desperate journey as a refugee in search of asylum appeared to be more of a jolly sightseeing holiday across Europe with friends. He had also left pornographic images on her computer.

Mohammed had said and done certain things that she couldn't get out of her mind—such as calling her "heartless." She wondered, "Was it heartless of me to take him in for six months? . . . In retrospect, I was so stupid, but also so arrogant. All my friends . . . kept warning me not to trust him, but I just thought: 'Oh, they're all racists, whereas I am this paragon of liberalism.' And I liked the idea that I was being 'daring' while they were being so cautious."

She concluded, "I've had almost a year to lick my wounds and now I think I'm ready to take another asylum seeker. I'll let you know how it goes."[1]

LESSONS FROM ASYLUM SEEKERS

One lesson from Lynn Barber's experience is that both secular fundamentalism and Islamic fundamentalism are caught in the grip of the delusion that the world could one day become a utopia if all competing worldviews were wiped off the map and everyone in the world thought and believed as they do.

Islamic fundamentalists want to do away with Christianity,

Israel, secularism, and Western civilization and impose a global caliphate on humanity. Many, if not most, secular fundamentalists want to do away with Christianity and seek to impose a utopia of rationalism, scientism, and atheism on humanity. Both the cult of Islam and the cult of secularism believe humanity could be perfected if they were allowed to impose their ideology on the human race.

The Christian faith does not claim it can bring about a utopia. Christianity rejects the delusion of Islamists and secular fundamentalists—the false notion that humanity can be perfected by ideology. As Christians, we are realistic about human nature. When we receive Christ as Lord and Savior, we are born again— *but we are not perfect people.* The absolute perfection of Jesus covers our sin, but the church is not a utopian community of sinless people. We are saved, but our old sin nature is still at work in us. That's why we identify with the anguished cry of the apostle Paul: "What a wretched man I am! Who will rescue me from this body that is subject to death?" (Romans 7:24).

It's true that humanity has made great strides in science and technology, but the human race is morally no more advanced than people were in the time of Noah. The belief in moral progress—an irrational belief held by both political progressives and religious progressives—is a mirage. There is no historical evidence that the human race is somehow learning from its past and becoming less hateful, less bigoted, less violent, and less warlike. All the evidence that we see in our history books, in our newspapers, and on our TV screens tells us that the human race is hopelessly mired in sin, just as the Bible has said all along. Though we would like to believe that humanity is moving toward a golden age of peace, love, and harmony, the reality is that we have been spinning our wheels in the mud and muck of sin for thousands of years.

In spite of all the evidence, many people discount the effects—and in some cases, even the existence—of sin, particularly in themselves. The Islamic fundamentalists don't blame their sin for the ills of the world; they blame the West, America, Christianity, and Israel for all that is wrong. And the secular fundamentalists don't blame sin for the ills of the world; they blame religion and intolerance. They reject the biblical truth about sin, which is a roadblock to utopia. As long as sin lives in us, humanity cannot be perfected—and the utopia dreamed of by the secular fundamentalists will be forever out of reach.

The story of Lynn Barber is also a microcosm of how Europe and Great Britain—and, to a lesser extent, the United States—have taken in refugees from the Middle East, knowing little or nothing about who they really are, where their allegiances lie, and whether they pose a danger to us. Since 2014, European nations have accepted vast numbers of Muslims from troubled regions, including Syria, Afghanistan, Iraq, and Nigeria. Once inside the European Union, many spread out into France, England, Germany, Austria, Hungary, and Scandinavia.

While it seems logical that many of the refugees from war zones would be women and children, a large percentage of these asylum seekers are young, healthy-looking men. Eurostat, the statistical analysis bureau of the European Union, reports that men far outnumbered women among first-time asylum applicants in 2015. Among applicants ages fourteen to thirty-four, three out of four were male; among applicants ages thirty-five to sixty-four, roughly three-fifths were male. These disturbing statistics show that European countries are importing large numbers of the key demographic group for Islamic terrorism—young Muslim men.[2]

Another question to consider: Why are Western countries expected to accept so many of the asylum seekers from the Middle East? From a cultural standpoint, wouldn't it make the most sense to send them to Arab countries where there would be no cultural or language barriers? Turkey, along with the Arab countries of Lebanon and Jordan, have taken in millions of refugees, but the rich Arab Gulf States that could easily afford to house refugees will not do so.

Over the past several years, we may have been witnessing a Muslim tradition known as *hijrah*, which literally means "migration." In AD 622, Muhammad led the first hijrah from Mecca to Medina. To this day, hijrah is a strategy for extending Islam into other lands. In fact, hijrah is sometimes called "jihad by migration." So the nations that invite these mostly male asylum seekers may be unwittingly importing jihad to their shores.[3]

Like Lynn Barber in her well-intentioned but ill-fated invitation to Mohammed, many Western governments are operating on illusions and delusions about the asylum seekers they allow into their borders. Illusions are deceptive. Delusions can lead us to destruction. Only the truth can save us from terrible mistakes that future generations will have to pay for.

DELUSIONS ABOUT ISLAMIC TERRORISM

On Monday, May 22, 2017, an Islamist suicide bomber detonated an explosive device packed with metal bolts in England's Manchester Arena just as an Ariana Grande pop music concert had ended and fans were streaming into the foyer. Twenty-two innocent people died, including an eight-year-old girl, Saffie Rose Roussos. The blast also injured 119 people, 23 of them critically.

The following morning, BBC news anchor Katty Kay told a TV audience, "Europe is getting used to attacks like this. [We] have to, because we are never going to be able to totally wipe this out. . . . We're going to see more of these kinds of attacks taking place in Europe."[4]

To me, this is a statement of defeatism. We in the West must not simply "get used to" a crescendoing, quickening drumbeat of terror attacks as our civilization disintegrates. We need to understand who stands at the gates of our society, with torches and battering rams in hand. We need to understand why they wish to kill us and our children, and why they wish to conquer our civilization.

Economist Thomas Piketty, author of *Capital in the 21st Century*, claims that radical Islamic terrorism is fueled by income inequality. "It's obvious," he said. "Terrorism feeds on the powder keg of Middle Eastern inequality, that we [the West] have largely contributed to creating."[5]

In 2015, State Department spokeswoman Marie Harf made a similar claim on MSNBC's *Hardball with Chris Matthews*. "We cannot win this fight by killing them [the terrorists]," she said. "We cannot kill our way out of this war. We need, in the . . . medium and longer term, to go after the root causes that lead people to join these groups, whether it's lack of opportunity for jobs—"

The host interrupted her, pointing out that some Muslims would always be impoverished.

"We can work with countries around the world to help . . . them build their economies so they can have job opportunities for these people," Harf responded.[6]

The naiveté of these two people—one a respected economist, the other a highly placed government spokeswoman—is nothing less than shocking. Clearly, they prize ideology above facts and objective truth. The solution to terrorism is *not* a jobs program. Why? Because the cause of terrorism is not poverty.

The truth is that some of the most infamous and deadly jihadist terrorists in recent years have been well-educated people who had no lack of economic opportunities. The most infamous of all, Al Qaeda founder Osama bin Laden, was the wealthy son of a billionaire construction industrialist. Osama bin Laden studied economics and business administration at King Abdulaziz University and may have earned his degree in civil engineering before pursuing a career in global terror. And bin Laden's successor, Ayman al-Zawahiri, came from a prosperous family of scholars and doctors; he studied medicine at Cairo University and served as a surgeon in the Egyptian Army.

A 2009 RAND Corporation study commissioned by the Department of Defense found that terrorists "are *not* particularly impoverished, uneducated, or afflicted by mental disease. . . . Terrorist leaders actually tend to come from relatively privileged backgrounds." And a 2002 study for the National Bureau of Economic Research found that both Hezbollah suicide bombers in Lebanon and Palestinian suicide bombers tended to be better educated and have better economic opportunities than their non-terrorist peers.[7]

A study of the root causes of terrorism by the World Bank concluded that ISIS members who volunteered to be suicide bombers tended to be educationally advantaged. The study examined 331 recruits from an ISIS membership database and found that 69 percent had at least a high school education, 25 percent had graduated from college, and the majority had jobs or careers at the time they joined ISIS. Being educated and having economic opportunities actually seemed to make these young men *more* likely to engage in terrorism and suicide bombings.

Also, a study by Britain's counterterrorism agency MI5 found that "two-thirds of the British suspects have a middle-class profile and those who want to become suicide bombers are often the most educated." Researchers have also found that ISIS terror recruits tend to come from the richest Islamic countries, not the poorest.[8]

Leftists want to believe that terrorism is a problem that can be solved with a government social program. That's how they might like to solve every social ill, from street crime to global terrorism: create a government program, throw millions or billions of dollars at the problem, and let the bureaucrats solve it. They believe in this solution as if it were their religion.

Terrorism is not caused by poverty. Terrorism is not caused by lack of education. Terrorism is caused by indoctrination into a radical ideology of Islamism. It is the young men of means in the Islamic society who can afford to be better educated, and it is the education they receive that initiates them into the ideology that drives them to commit such gruesome acts.

Whenever the bloodthirsty barbarians of Al Qaeda or Boko Haram or ISIS commit some horrifying atrocity, politicians and media pundits are quick to rush in front of the television cameras and explain that the terrorists are not truly Islamic—they represent a "perversion" of Islam. They want us all to understand that "Islam is a religion of peace."

They either don't understand the truth about Islam or are deliberately misrepresenting the reality—and they have an emotional need to be seen as open-minded, tolerant, and enlightened.

There are certain centers of influence in America where leftist ideology tends to be concentrated: the marble halls of the District of Columbia; the news studios of New York, Washington, and Atlanta; the TV and motion picture studios of Hollywood; and the major university campuses across the nation. Within these leftist enclaves, "Islamophilia" (embracing and loving Islam and Muslims) is one of the greatest virtues—and "Islamophobia" (fear or distrust of Islam and Muslims) is one of the greatest sins. Anyone in these leftist communities who is even faintly suspected of Islamophobia will be purged and shunned.

Very few people have the courage to stand alone for the truth. Most just want to belong. Most just want to be a part of the community. Most just want to conform. In general, people are scared of being the pariah, of losing their friends, their social standing, or their jobs. People will go to any extreme to prove they belong among the elite and the enlightened. In the case of those on the left, this means embracing Islam.

What is the truth about radical, militant, political Islam? What is the truth about terrorist groups like Al Qaeda, Boko Haram, and ISIS? Have they truly "perverted" Islam? Is *genuine* Islam a "religion of peace," as so many of our leaders would have us believe?

I was born in Egypt, the son of Christian parents in an overwhelmingly Islamic culture. Most of my friends in school were Muslims. Over the years, I have had many conversations with Muslims, including Islamist hard-liners. And I can tell you, confidently and with firsthand assurance, that there truly are moderate Muslims who want only to live in peace with Americans and with Westerners in general. Yet often their values and outlook conflict with ours.

The truth is, many moderate Muslims would not pick up the

phone to stop the next terrorist attack. Even if they knew an attack was about to take place, they wouldn't risk reporting the plot to the police. They would be afraid of being the next to be targeted.

According to a 2016 scientific poll commissioned by Britain's Channel 4, two-thirds of British Muslims said they would not tell police if they knew someone who was involved with a terrorist organization (though a majority said they would try to dissuade them personally or find someone else in the community who would). And about one-third of Muslims polled would not condemn those who used violence against people who insulted the Prophet Muhammad. Some would probably say, "*I* wouldn't kill anybody, but I'm okay with it when *other* people do." And nearly one-fourth favored the introduction of Sharia law in England.

Trevor Phillips, former chairman of the Equality and Human Rights Commission, said that the poll revealed "the unacknowledged creation of a nation within the nation, with its own geography, its own values, and its own very separate future." He added that he had long thought that "Europe's Muslims would become like previous waves of migrants, gradually abandoning their ancestral ways, wearing their religious and cultural baggage lightly, and gradually blending into Britain's diverse identity landscape."[9] But the poll had proved him wrong.

As disturbing as these findings may be, I want to state that I am a Christian Islamophile. That is, I am a person who loves Muslims with the love of Jesus. I believe their religion is false and their worldview is broken, and I want them to encounter the Savior who declared, "I am the way and the truth and the life. No one comes to the Father except through me" (John 14:6). I am 100 percent convinced of what the apostle Peter said when he testified before the Sanhedrin: "Salvation is found in no one else, for there is no other name under heaven given to mankind by which we must be saved" (Acts 4:12). I would not be true to my Lord and Savior, Jesus Christ, if I believed otherwise.

But I do not look down on the Muslim people. I love them. I am burdened for them. I pray for them. And the reason I am so heartbroken over the Muslim people is that I know the truth about their religion. The terrorists of Al Qaeda, Boko Haram, and ISIS do not represent a "perversion" of Islam. They represent a particular *interpretation* of Islam's holy book, the Qur'an.

The Qur'an contains many passages that speak of peace, but also a number that speak of going to war against "unbelievers." One verse often cited by the terrorists is Qur'an 8:12: "When your Lord revealed to the angels: I am with you, therefore make firm those who believe. I will cast terror into the hearts of those who disbelieve. Therefore strike off their heads and strike off every fingertip of them."[10]

So when the terrorists go to war against "those who disbelieve" in Islam, when they commit beheadings and other atrocities, they are not "perverting" Islam. They are following the tenets of the Qur'an, faithfully and literally, as they interpret it. The terrorists themselves would certainly never say they are corrupting their faith. They would say they are practicing it with absolute fidelity.

The foot soldiers of radical Islam are completely dedicated to their cause—and they have nothing but contempt for those in the West who they assume are led by their feelings. The terrorists operate by a cold-blooded reality. They believe that we in the West have gone soft, that we are weak and all too willing to submit to the sword of Islam. I fear they may be right.

Many of our leaders seem desperate to be liked by our adversaries, the media, or the voters. Few seem determined to stand for the truth, whatever the cost, no matter how unpopular it may be. America's adversaries in the Middle East and around the world know that many of our leaders operate from a "trust your feelings" mind-set. Our adversaries know how to use this weakness to their own advantage. That's why America has lost the trust of the world as a guardian and guarantor of international order and stability.

THE "LIVING DOCUMENT" DELUSION

The left's preference for "progress" and tolerance extends to the way they view America's founding documents. Given that the views of so many of our leaders shift depending on how the political winds are blowing—all in the name of tolerance—it's not surprising that many liberal thinkers view the US Constitution as a "living document." As a result, they aren't bound by what the Constitution literally says and originally meant. We saw this attitude expressed by Senator Dianne Feinstein of California during the Supreme Court confirmation hearings for Judge Neil Gorsuch in March 2017. Senator Feinstein said,

> I firmly believe the American Constitution is a living document intended to evolve as our country evolves. In 1789, the population of the United States was under four million. Today, we're 325 million and growing. At the time of our founding, African Americans were enslaved. It was not so long after women had been burned at the stake for witchcraft. And the idea of an automobile, let alone the Internet, was unfathomable. In fact, if we were to dogmatically adhere to "originalist" interpretations, then we would still have segregated schools and bans on

interracial marriage. Women wouldn't be entitled to equal protection under the law. And government discrimination against LGBT Americans would be permitted.[11]

Senator Feinstein was stating a view that I believe is simply ridiculous (to put it charitably). Her claim that an originalist interpretation of the Constitution would impose segregation on schools and marriage, as well as discrimination against LGBT Americans is absurd. The Constitution, as written, does not require any such thing. And as for equal protection for women, states were allowed under the original Constitution to permit women to vote. In 1920, the Nineteenth Amendment guaranteed *all* women in *every* state the right to cast ballots, but prior to 1920, women were already allowed to vote in a number of states.

We all agree that it should be possible to change the Constitution as society changes. The difference between conservatives and liberals like Senator Feinstein is that conservatives believe the Constitution should be changed only by the amendment process clearly spelled out in article 5 of the Constitution. Senator Feinstein and others who view the Constitution as "living" want to give the awesome power to change the meaning of the Constitution to nine unelected Supreme Court justices. We saw the destructive power of that approach to altering the Constitution in January 1973, in the case of *Roe v. Wade*, when seven black-robed men (out of nine justices) took it upon themselves to overturn laws restricting abortion in every state of the Union. That decision opened deep wounds and divisions in our national psyche that have not healed to this day.

But before coming down too hard on progressive politicians and their followers, we have to ask: What about the church? Like

America, the Christian church is divided between right and left, between a traditional, conservative, orthodox wing and a liberal, progressive wing. Former president Barack Obama is a notable example of someone who embraces liberal Christianity.

For twenty years, he sat under the liberal teaching of his Chicago pastor, Jeremiah Wright, who once thundered from his pulpit, "The government gives [African Americans] the drugs, builds bigger prisons, passes a three-strike law and then wants us to sing 'God Bless America.' No." He went on to suggest—using colorful language—that America should be condemned for killing innocent people.[12]

In 2004, *Chicago Sun-Times* religion columnist Cathleen Falsani interviewed Barack Obama, then an Illinois state senator, about his religious beliefs. Senator Obama said, "I am a Christian. So, I have a deep faith. So I draw from the Christian faith." He then talked about being influenced by Eastern religion, Islam, and Judaism, concluding, "I believe that there are many paths to the same place"[13]—a direct rejection of the Christianity of Christ himself, who said, "*No one* comes to the Father *except through me*" (John 14:6, emphasis added).

Bible-believing Christians cannot accept the "many paths" view as a genuine expression of their faith. Yet the Christian left considers this "inclusive" stance to be the enlightened one. Liberal Christianity offers a humanistic reinterpretation of our faith and claims that Bible-believing Christians are mired in rigid, unenlightened, antiquated thinking. They tell us that times have changed, society has progressed, and the church must evolve to keep up.

In 2012, when President Obama was explaining his rationale for changing his position on same-sex marriage, he framed that rationale in the context of his professed Christian faith. He said, "When I read the Bible, I do so with the belief that it is not a static text but the Living Word and that I must continually be open to new revelations." He appears to be saying that the Bible is a "living document" that may be radically reinterpreted—so that its original meaning is turned upside down!—as society and opinions change.[14]

Now, this is a subtle and clever twist on the word *living*. The Bible itself says, "The word of God is alive and active. Sharper than any double-edged sword, it penetrates even to dividing soul and spirit, joints and marrow; it judges the thoughts and attitudes of the heart" (Hebrews 4:12). And Martin Luther once said, "The Bible is alive, it speaks to me; it has feet, it runs after me; it has hands, it lays hold of me." But neither the writer of Hebrews nor Martin Luther meant that the Bible is subject to revision or "new revelations" according to shifting public tastes and political moods.

The Bible doesn't change; it changes us. If we disagree with something we read in Scripture, it's not the Bible that needs to change—it's us. We must reexamine our opinions and change them in the light of God's unchanging Word.

As various leaders and authors in the church subtly move away from a biblical understanding of social issues, the church is being led into apostasy and error, while the nation is being led into secularism, moral relativism, and depravity. The church has surrendered its role of influence in the public square and in the national conversation. The church has sidelined itself and made itself irrelevant at the very time that the world is in desperate need of God's truth.

Apostasy in today's church takes many forms, including some

bodies that label themselves "evangelical." Many of these movements, which are defined on pages 116–117, ask the same question Pontius Pilate asked before handing Jesus over to the mob: "What is truth?" (John 18:38). Jesus saw the dismissive attitude behind Pilate's question and refused to answer him. Christ taught His disciples the importance of knowing, speaking, and defending the truth because Jesus Himself is Truth incarnate.

God's message to us hasn't changed since the beginning of time. It remains the same: Do not tamper with the truth of God. On the Day of Judgment, religious leaders who have betrayed God's truth will receive the harshest condemnation.

Christian complacency and apostasy are a far greater threat to the life of the church than ISIS or any other terrorist group. The church cannot be conquered from without by any of them. The church can only be destroyed from within if we stray from the Scriptures and contaminate God's truth with worldly ideas. The church must wake up and shake itself from its long stupor.

You and I and everyone who claims to follow Jesus must take an unshakable stand on the unchanging Truth.

ACTIVISTS FOR APOSTASY

In perhaps no other area are Christians facing more pressure to compromise God's Word than the issue of gay marriage and LGBT rights. In July 2014, the *Atlantic* published a story of how the LGBT agenda is being smuggled into evangelical Christian colleges across the nation. It's a stealth strategy to radically alter what these schools teach about homosexuality. The authors focused on Gordon College in Massachusetts, a school founded in 1889 by A. J. Gordon to train and equip young people to proclaim God's truth (the school was originally called Boston Missionary Training School):

> When we, the authors, attended Gordon College over a decade ago, the vast majority of administrators, faculty, and students simply assumed that the Bible prohibited same-sex attraction. Nestled on Boston's North Shore, this small outpost of evangelical Protestantism taught us that it was wrong to be gay—not just wrong, but explicitly condemned by both God and the college code of conduct. Sure, a fledgling group emerged here and there to foster dialogue about homosexuality and Christian faith, exploring the edges of accepted belief, but all of us—questioners and Bible-thumpers alike—signed an agreement, stating in no uncertain terms that we would not take part in homosexual activities of any kind.[15]

Did the school really teach that it is "wrong" to be gay in the sense that God condemns people with homosexual tendencies and temptations? I doubt that. There is no passage of Scripture in which God condemns people for having homosexual tendencies or for having a same-sex attraction. What *clearly* is condemned in Scripture is (1) engaging in sexual activity, whether homosexual or heterosexual, outside the secure and God-ordained enclosure of marriage; and (2) promoting and advocating sexual sin. That is what Paul tells us:

> God gave them over in the sinful desires of their hearts to sexual impurity for the degrading of their bodies with one another. They exchanged the truth about God for a lie,

and worshiped and served created things rather than the
Creator—who is forever praised. Amen.

Because of this, God gave them over to shameful lusts.
Even their women exchanged natural sexual relations for
unnatural ones. In the same way the men also abandoned
natural relations with women and were inflamed with
lust for one another. Men committed shameful acts with
other men, and received in themselves the due penalty
for their error.

ROMANS 1:24-27

This is not a question of "exploring the edges of accepted
belief," as if there is some ambiguity or alternate interpretation of
what the Bible says about all forms of sexual impurity. We must
either accept God's Word as truth—or reject it.

The *Atlantic* piece goes on to say that a Gordon alum quietly
founded a group called OneGordon—"a student and alumni
LGBT alliance"—in 2012 as an avenue for dialogue and as an
advocacy group to pressure college administrators to change their
interpretation of Scripture and conform to political correctness.

The authors point out that evangelical Christians make up
approximately 28 percent of the US population and are, as they
put it, "still the largest voting block opposing equal rights for
LGBT people." But the authors celebrate the fact that evangelicals are no longer united in their belief that Scripture reserves
sexual activity to marriages between a man and a woman (see
Mark 10:6-9; Ephesians 5:31-32). In 2004, they say, only about a
tenth of evangelicals supported gay marriage versus about a quar-
ter of evangelicals in 2014—and a near majority of evangelicals
under age thirty-five (according to the Public Religion Research

Institute). "If this trend continues," the authors conclude, "it is not an exaggeration to say that the most formidable obstruction to gay rights in the United States will dissolve."

They welcome this, of course, as a *good* thing. Those of us who stand firmly on God's Word know that it is a sign of growing apostasy. God established marriage between a man and a woman as a picture of the union between Christ and His bride, the church. LGBT activists have figured out how to encourage compromise in the church in order to gain acceptance for their beliefs and grow their own political power.

Though the *Atlantic* article focuses on the activities of OneGordon, a Google search shows that LGBT activist groups are infiltrating other Christian campuses, hoping to turn those institutions away from God's truth and going by names like OneBiola, OneGeorgeFox, OneWheaton, OneWestmont, Cedarville Out, BJUnity (Bob Jones University), SPU Haven (Seattle Pacific University), and more. As the *Atlantic* authors observe, "Most future evangelical pastors, theologians, and leaders will be graduates" of the approximately 120 Christian schools that belong to the Council for Christian Colleges and Universities (with a combined student body of more than 400,000). These activists hope to radically alter how God's Word will be taught from church pulpits for generations to come. I see this as a satanic strategy designed to accelerate the spread of apostasy by striking at the heart of Christian higher learning.

I don't hate homosexual activists and lobbyists, and I wish them no harm. But we must spread the word about their agenda, and we must use every righteous means to prevent them from implementing a strategy of exchanging the truth of God for a lie. Through prayer, through courageously contending for the truth, and through tirelessly maintaining a watchful vigil over Christian colleges and universities, we can keep the preaching of God's Word strong.

We have to stop being afraid of being labeled "haters" and "bigots." The world is counting on our timidity in the face of name-calling and opposition. If we fear anything, let us only be afraid of disappointing the Lord and losing our distinctiveness as Christians.

MURDERED BY ILLUSIONS

Otto Warmbier was an athletic and studious junior at the University of Virginia who was working toward a double major in commerce and economics. In December 2015, he was on his way to a study-abroad program in Hong Kong when he saw a travel company's advertisement for trips to North Korea. The tour company promised "budget travel to destinations your mother would rather you stayed away from. . . . Fun, thrill seeking and adventure at a great price."[16] Otto was adventurous and liked to see new places. He had already toured Israel and completed an exchange program with the London School of Economics. Intrigued by the chance to visit another country, Warmbier booked a five-day tour of North Korea.

He befriended a man from Britain, Danny Gratton, and they roomed together at the Yanggakdo International Hotel in Pyongyang. Warmbier enjoyed the tour and was planning to visit Beijing next. On the second night of his stay, he is said to have taken a propaganda poster from the hotel as a souvenir. Removing a poster from a hotel wall in the United States would not be considered a major offense. But this poster featured the image of the late North Korean dictator Kim Jong-Il and a patriotic slogan. Warmbier was unaware that taking an item with the image of the supreme leader is a serious crime in that country.

On January 2, 2016, Warmbier was preparing to leave North Korea from Pyongyang International Airport. He was in a boarding line with Gratton when two North Korean guards tapped him on the shoulder and led him away. Neither Warmbier nor Gratton thought there was a serious problem. Gratton joked, "Well, we won't be seeing you again." Otto smiled back as he walked away with the guards.

But Gratton's joke proved bitterly ironic. The tour group departed on time—but Otto Warmbier remained in North Korea, charged with committing a "hostile act" against the state. He was tried, convicted, and sentenced to fifteen years of hard labor in a North Korean prison.

Warmbier's father appealed to the Obama administration for help in obtaining the young man's release. The officials Mr. Warmbier spoke with urged him to keep a low profile, avoid the media, and say nothing. They had a term for that approach: "strategic patience." It was a phrase the Obama administration used to describe its seeming inaction toward oppressive and dangerous regimes in North Korea, Iran, Syria, Venezuela, and elsewhere.[17] Avoid doing anything or saying anything that might upset the dictators. Be patient. It's all part of the strategy.

Mr. Warmbier reluctantly agreed to allow time for this approach to work. Months passed. The Obama administration left office, and the Trump administration came in, announcing that the era of "strategic patience" was over. Finally, Mr. Warmbier hoped he might see his son again.

No one knew that not long after Otto Warmbier's sentencing,

something happened to this young man that caused him to suffer severe brain damage. His family will probably never know the exact cause of their son's injury, other than that it was a horrible act perpetrated by his captors.

The Trump administration worked for Otto Warmbier's release, and Mr. Warmbier and his wife made media appearances to make the public aware that their son was being held in North Korean captivity. Finally, after seventeen months in a North Korean prison, Otto Warmbier was released—but he was in an irreversible coma. Doctors who examined him upon his return to America described him as being in "a state of unresponsive wakefulness." Whatever the North Korean government had done to him caused extensive brain damage.

Otto's parents were not prepared for their reunion with their son at Cincinnati's Lunken Airport. They pictured Otto being asleep, resting quietly in a medically induced coma. Otto's actual condition was beyond comprehension.

"We walked over to the plane," Otto's father, Fred, recalled. "When we got halfway up the steps we heard this howling, involuntary, inhuman sound. We weren't really certain what it was." When they saw Otto, he was jerking violently on a stretcher and crying out like a wounded animal. His head was shaved and he stared blankly. "He was blind. He was deaf. . . . It looked like someone had taken a pair of pliers and rearranged his bottom teeth."[18]

Moments after seeing Otto for the first time, his anguished mother and sister ran off the plane. "They destroyed him," his mother later said.[19] Over the next few days, Otto's parents and siblings surrounded him, touched him, and spoke lovingly to him. Within a day, his countenance changed. His family said they could see that he was at peace. He seemed to know that he was home.[20]

Six days after his arrival in the United States, on the afternoon of June 19, 2017, Otto died at the age of twenty-two. As Senator John McCain said shortly after the young man's death, "Otto Warmbier . . . was murdered by the Kim Jong-un regime."[21]

But Otto Warmbier also died as a result of misconceptions, of being unaware of certain truths. The travel company sold him an illusion of "fun, thrill seeking and adventure at a great price" and did not mention the risks of making any misstep in that rigidly controlled communist society. He was under the illusion that he could simply take a poster from the hotel wall as a souvenir without any consequences. And the Obama administration was under the illusion that so-called "strategic patience"—saying and doing little while hoping that things would turn out all right—was actually a strategy.

As dramatic and horrifying as Otto's story is, Americans have also been living with delusions for decades. We have been under the illusion that we could allow rogue nations like North Korea and Iran to build up their nuclear programs, and we wouldn't be threatened. We have been under the illusion that we could simply ignore Islamic fundamentalism, and it would leave us alone. (That illusion was shattered on September 11, 2001.) We have been under the illusion that we could "compromise" on moral issues, and the secularists would be satisfied and not try to silence us any longer. These are frightening illusions. These are deadly delusions. They threaten to topple our civilization.

Western civilization is in a state of unresponsive wakefulness. We are culturally comatose. Only one thing can save us: a massive injection of the truth . . .

If it's not already too late.

IS GOD'S JUDGMENT INEVITABLE?

HOW WILL AMERICA DIE?

That's a grim question, and probably not one you wish to think about. But the death of America is a very real possibility. If we want America to remain a land of freedom, opportunity, and security for our children and grandchildren, then we need to ask ourselves in all seriousness, How will America die?

If you ask secular futurists and doomsayers what kinds of threats keep them awake at night, they'll probably say they worry about pandemic diseases, biological terrorism, the nuclear threat, cyber attacks, race wars, or even an asteroid crashing to Earth from outer space.

But if you ask historians and Bible scholars what keeps them awake at night, they'll say they worry about the lessons of history and of Scripture. Most will say they think about the fall of Israel and Judah, when the Assyrians and Babylonians carried out God's judgment by taking these kingdoms captive. They'll say they think about the fall of Rome. Once the most powerful and prosperous empire on earth, Rome was decaying from within because of immorality and corruption long before its collapse. Historian Edward McNall Burns observes that during the reign of Emperor Trajan in the early second century, Rome was famed for its great wealth and even greater depravity: "There were 32,000 prostitutes in Rome during the reign of Trajan, and . . . homosexuality was exceedingly common and even fashionable."[1]

As barbarian hordes were conquering the Roman Empire in the fifth century, a Roman Christian writer named Salvian lamented, "We are right now being overcome solely by the impurity of our vices. . . . You, O Roman people, be ashamed; be ashamed of your lives."[2]

David M. Walker, the former comptroller general of the United States, warns in his book *Comeback America* that the collapse of the Roman Empire may well be a foreshadowing of our own future:

> Americans tend not to pay much attention to the lessons
> of history. Well, we should start, because those lessons
> are brutal. . . . Many of us think that a superpowerful,
> prosperous nation like America will be a permanent
> fixture dominating the world scene. We are too big
> to fail. But you don't have to delve far into the history
> books to see what has happened to other once-dominant
> powers. . . .
>
> The millennium of the Roman Empire—which
> included five hundred years as a republic—came to an
> end in the fifth century after scores of years of gradual
> decay. . . . America presents unsettling parallels with
> the disintegration of Rome—a decline of moral values,
> a loss of political civility, an overextended military, an

inability to control national borders, and the growth of fiscal irresponsibility by the central government. Do these sound familiar?[3]

And historian Niall Ferguson warns that when a civilization dies, the death throes can occur without warning and with astonishing swiftness:

> What is most striking about this . . . history is the speed of the Roman Empire's collapse. In just five decades, the population of Rome itself fell by three-quarters. Archaeological evidence from the late fifth century— inferior housing, more primitive pottery, fewer coins, smaller cattle—shows that the benign influence of Rome diminished rapidly in the rest of Western Europe. . . . "The end of civilization" came within the span of a single generation.
>
> Other great empires have suffered comparably swift collapses. . . . [Empires] function in apparent equilibrium for some unknowable period. And then, quite abruptly, they collapse. . . . The shift . . . to destruction and then to desolation is not cyclical. It is sudden.[4]

Bible teacher Warren W. Wiersbe reflects on the lessons we can learn from the Jewish exiles to Babylon in the sixth century BC and places them in the context of the moral and spiritual corruption that has infested the American church:

> How easy it is for us today to pass judgment on God's ancient people, but what about God's contemporary

people? Sexual sins in the church and in so-called Christian homes have ripped churches and families apart, and many churches close their eyes to these offenses. Pornography—in print, on video, and on the Internet—is a common thing these days, and it's getting more and more daring on television. Unmarried people living together, "trial marriages," "gay marriages," and even "mate-swapping" have shown up in evangelical churches, and when faithful pastors have attempted to deal with such sin, they were told to mind their own business. The offenders simply left and started attending other churches where they could live as they pleased. As Ruth Bell Graham said, "If God doesn't judge America, He will have to apologize to Sodom and Gomorrah."[5]

These are sobering words, and they should trouble not only our sleep but our waking hours as well. Anyone who thinks that America is immortal and invulnerable to decline and collapse has never studied the lessons of history—especially biblical history. Nothing lasts forever, and that includes the United States of America.

So how do *you* think America will die?

Do you think America can be saved?

"DID GOD REALLY SAY . . . ?"

I don't believe America has to die in our generation. Yet the level of immorality and apostasy in the American church today must certainly break God's heart. As I look around at all the warning signs in the church and our surrounding culture, I can't help feeling that we are close—perilously close—to the point of no return. Still I believe and hope and pray, for the sake of our children and grandchildren, that repentance and healing are still within our reach.

I don't want to be here when God finally decides, "Enough is enough," and America goes the way of ancient Israel and the Roman Empire. We who bear the name of Christ must wake up and shake ourselves from our long stupor. We must recommit ourselves to standing for God's truth. We must rededicate ourselves to taking the great commission seriously and taking the good news of Jesus Christ to the world around us, starting with our next-door neighbors and reaching out to the ends of the earth. Instead of accommodating ourselves to the lies of our culture, we must proactively teach and preach the truth of the gospel to this dying world, including the secularists and Muslims whose worldviews are so different from ours.

When believers strayed from God's truth in the seventh century, they opened the door for the false religion of Muhammad. Today, we are once again hearing distorted "gospels" from people who claim to speak for Christ, who even call themselves evangelicals, but who have compromised the truth of God's Word.

As a pastor, trained and ordained in the Anglican Church (also known as the Episcopal Church or the Church of England), I have seen the damage done when church leaders began preaching a false gospel under the guise of "rescuing the gospel from fundamentalists." Biblical, evangelical Anglicanism has a rich history that began in the sixteenth and seventeenth centuries with such outstanding leaders as Thomas Cranmer, Richard Hooker, and Lancelot Andrewes. That history continues to this century, through such faithful evangelical Anglicans as J. I. Packer, Alister McGrath, and the late John R. W. Stott. Yet there is no denying that, as a general trend, the leaders of the Church of England have taken the denomination away from fidelity to the Word of God.

In 2015, the Archbishops of Canterbury and York issued a statement warning that the Church of England was rapidly losing membership and that attendance on a typical Sunday was *half* of what it had been in 1975. As a result, the church faced a crisis of precarious finances, an inability to attract, train, and retain clergy, and an inability to maintain aging church buildings.[6]

While a faithful, Bible-believing remnant remains in the Anglican church, the denomination's drift toward apostasy and irrelevancy is the principal reason that I, as a pastor, and my congregation, The Church Of The Apostles, are no longer affiliated with the Anglican church. The reasons for the Church of England's loss of membership should be obvious to Anglican leaders, because it is right there in the Scriptures, in the words of Jesus in Matthew 5:13: "You are the salt of the earth. But if the salt loses its saltiness, how can it be made salty again?" When a denomination loses its saltiness, people stop attending its churches.

In recent years, I have seen a similar movement toward apostasy and irrelevancy sweeping across much of evangelicalism. Many once-evangelical leaders and churches are losing their saltiness. I cringe when I hear pastors and authors (or pastors who are authors) deny orthodox positions on heaven or hell, the purpose of the Cross, the meaning of marriage, and the authority of Scripture. These leaders often seem driven by a desire for inclusivity and "sensitivity to people's feelings" rather than a desire to be faithful to God's Word. In fact, many argue that Scripture needs to be contextualized in light of today's culture, so they present their positions as new, more informed viewpoints better suited to the challenges we face in today's world. Ironically, their sermons and books are nothing but the same old set of heresies dressed up in postmodern jargon. At its heart, every heresy challenges or rejects Christ's nature and position within the Godhead, the meaning of the Cross, and/or the authority of Scripture.

Another feature of these teachers' postmodern musings on Scripture and the nature of God: Their reflections offer few certainties about God's truth, but they do raise a lot of questions. It reminds me of the tone of the serpent in Eden, who asked Eve, "Did God really say . . . ?"

Down through history, the Church of Jesus Christ has always been strengthened, emboldened, and energized by recognizing the uncompromised truth of God's Word—revelation that points to Christ as the One who reconciles us to God. And whenever the church has begun to stray from that truth, compromise that truth, and replace that truth with man-made doctrines, the result has been decline and death. When churches chased after heresies in the seventh and eighth centuries, those churches became corpses—hollowed-out husks of their former selves. It wasn't hard for the armies of militant Islam to march across North Africa, up into the Holy Land and beyond, filling the vacuum left by so many dead churches.

There are many parallels between those days and our own time. Too many people within the church have willingly set aside their orthodox Christian beliefs to embrace a more progressive, "tolerant" view of God and Scripture. Heresies and false gospels are once again on the rise in the evangelical church—and militant Islam is once again on the march. Our own post-truth world is the perfect breeding ground for both Christian heresies and Islamic extremism. In centuries past, militant Islam failed in its attempt to conquer the world—because the church rediscovered God's truth in time.

Will the church of the twenty-first century wake up to the truth before Western civilization sinks into moral and spiritual collapse? What does God's Word say we must do to rescue the church from God's judgment? Is it too late for us to return to God, to humble ourselves, pray, and turn from our wicked ways?

WHAT THE BIBLE SAYS TO US ABOUT GOD'S JUDGMENT

God takes sin, corruption, and violence very seriously. We see this in the account of Noah and the flood:

> Now the earth was corrupt in God's sight and was full of violence. God saw how corrupt the earth had become, for all the people on earth had corrupted their ways. So God said to Noah, "I am going to put an end to all people, for the earth is filled with violence because of them. I am surely going to destroy both them and the earth."
>
> GENESIS 6:11-13

God is also offended when human beings rebel against Him and arrogantly seek to replace the worship of God with the worship of self. That is what happened in the account of the tower of Babel. Many people misunderstand the story, thinking that the people of Babel—the early Babylonians—were trying to build an immense tower that would enable them to walk up a spiral staircase right into heaven. That's not what the account says:

> They said, "Come, let us build ourselves a city, with a tower that reaches to the heavens, so that we may make a name for ourselves; otherwise we will be scattered over the face of the whole earth."

GENESIS 11:4

It's not the *height* of the tower that is significant in this passage. It's the *purpose* of the tower. The Babylonians were building the tower of Babel as *a monument to their own brilliance and glory*. They wanted the tower to establish their fame throughout the world. They were narcissists, obsessed with the worship and glorification of the self. They had replaced the worship of God with self-worship. This is one of the first mentions of Babylon in Scripture. Throughout the rest of the Old and New Testaments, all the way to the book of Revelation, Babylon stands as a symbol for self-centered enmity with God.

As you may recall, Israel was united from about 1050 BC to 930 BC. At that point, the country divided into a northern kingdom (Israel) and a southern kingdom (Judah). Both fell into apostasy, and God eventually led His people into exile. The northern kingdom was conquered by the Assyrians in about 722 BC. When God needed to discipline and judge Judah for the sin of spiritual adultery and apostasy about 150 years later, He chose the Babylonians as the instrument of His judgment. God used King Nebuchadnezzar of Babylon as His rod of discipline against Judah. Why? Because King Nebuchadnezzar was a self-aggrandizing, self-deifying, narcissistic ruler who imagined himself a god. He demanded that everyone in the kingdom bow down to his image.

When the Last Days come upon the earth, the Antichrist will be a man very much like King Nebuchadnezzar, a self-aggrandizing, self-deifying, narcissistic dictator who sets up his own image in the Temple of the Lord (the prophet Daniel called this image "an abomination that causes desolation" [Daniel 9:27]). He will demand that everyone in the world bow down to his image.

Today, in our own society, we are repeating the pattern of Babylon. Our culture is riddled with self-worship and enmity toward God. Our government has erased God from the public square. Our entertainment media have replaced all references to God with secularism and so-called "political correctness." Western civilization is aligning itself with the idolatry of Babylon, just as Israel once aligned itself with the idolatry of the Canaanites and other pagan nations. Whenever a civilization exchanges the worship of God for the idolatry of the self, it invites fear, terror, and judgment.

I believe the seething hatred and terrorism that breeds and grows across North Africa, the Middle East, and Asia is a foreshadowing of God's approaching judgment. If we spiritually and morally align ourselves with Babylon, we invite God to deal with us exactly as He dealt with ancient Israel.

The Babylonian conquerors brought a message to the people of Israel—a message from God Himself. Through the army of Nebuchadnezzar, God was telling His people, "The pagans hate Me and reject Me and worship false gods—yet you want to be like them. Have it your own way. I am removing My hand of protection from you. The Babylonians—the people who hated Me and defied Me and started building a tower to glorify and deify themselves—are now at your gates, ready to lead you away in chains."

What is the message God has for us today? And who is the messenger God is sending to us? Could it be that the young ISIS militant who seeks our destruction is really God's instrument to get our attention? I pray that we come to our senses in time to spare our children and grandchildren such terrors.

I love the beautiful promise contained in 2 Chronicles 7:14, which begins, "If my people, who are called by my name . . ." It's a wonderful promise—but it's important that we understand this promise in context. God made this promise to King Solomon soon after he had completed the construction of the great Temple in Jerusalem. God said,

> I have heard your prayer and have chosen this place for myself as a temple for sacrifices.
>
> When I shut up the heavens so that there is no rain, or command locusts to devour the land or send a plague among my people, if my people, who are called by my name, will humble themselves and pray and seek my face and turn from their wicked ways, then I will hear from heaven, and I will forgive their sin and will heal their land. Now my eyes will be open and my ears attentive to the prayers offered in this place. I have chosen and consecrated this temple so that my Name may be there forever. My eyes and my heart will always be there.
>
> As for you, if you walk before me faithfully as David your father did, and do all I command, and observe my decrees and laws, I will establish your royal throne, as I covenanted with David your father when I said, "You shall never fail to have a successor to rule over Israel."
>
> But if you turn away and forsake the decrees and commands I have given you and go off to serve other gods and worship them, then I will uproot Israel from my land,

which I have given them, and will reject this temple I have consecrated for my Name. I will make it a byword and an object of ridicule among all peoples. This temple will become a heap of rubble. All who pass by will be appalled and say, "Why has the LORD done such a thing to this land and to this temple?" People will answer, "Because they have forsaken the LORD, the God of their ancestors, who brought them out of Egypt, and have embraced other gods, worshiping and serving them—that is why he brought all this disaster on them."

2 CHRONICLES 7:12-22

If we Christians, who are called by His name, would humble ourselves and repent of our sins, I believe God would forgive our sin and heal our land. (Yes, I believe this promise applies to America just as it applied to ancient Israel.) God would heal us from the scourge of terrorism. He would heal us from the unsustainable national debt that threatens to collapse our economy. He would heal us from race hatred, crime, drug abuse, alcoholism, and all the other social ills that afflict our society. He would heal us from atheism, secularism, and the mockery of God that pollutes our media. But His promise comes with a warning: If we are unfaithful to the Lord, if we stray from the faith and worship other gods, disaster will follow.

Shortly before God's judgment fell upon the northern kingdom of Israel in the form of Assyrian invaders, God warned Israel through the prophet Hosea, "The people have broken my covenant and rebelled against my law" (Hosea 8:1).

The people protested, "Our God, we acknowledge you!" (verse 2).

But God replied, "Israel has rejected what is good; an enemy will pursue him. They set up kings without my consent; they choose princes without my approval. With their silver and gold they make idols for themselves to their own destruction" (verses 3-4). The people thought they acknowledged God, but God told them they were unfaithful.

So we have to ask ourselves, Are we, as Christians in the twenty-first century, unfaithful to God as well? Have we substituted a worldly religion in place of the purity of God's Word? That's the warning the apostle Paul sounded when he wrote to the church in Corinth:

> I am jealous for you with a godly jealousy. I promised you to one husband, to Christ, so that I might present you as a pure virgin to him. But I am afraid that just as Eve was deceived by the serpent's cunning, your minds may somehow be led astray from your sincere and pure devotion to Christ. For if someone comes to you and preaches a Jesus other than the Jesus we preached, or if you receive a different spirit from the Spirit you received, or a different gospel from the one you accepted, you put up with it easily enough.
>
> 2 CORINTHIANS 11:2-4

When Paul speaks of a "sincere and pure devotion to Christ," the idea behind "sincere devotion" in the Greek is the word *haplotēs*, which literally means "singleness" and "simplicity." It would, for instance, apply to clear, pure drinking water without additives or pollutants. And I think it's important that Paul, like the Old Testament prophets, uses the image of marriage to suggest the relationship between God and His people. He tells us that if we receive a "different gospel," we are committing spiritual adultery.

The good news of Jesus Christ is transparently clear—yet we have adulterated it with false ideologies and man-made doctrines. Some would have us believe that the good news of the Bible is "love wins"—that is, Jesus' sacrifice was unnecessary because God will ultimately let everyone into His Kingdom—but I believe that is the kind of "different gospel" Paul warned us against. The clear, pure, unadulterated gospel that we find in the Bible is simply this: Jesus died, Jesus arose, Jesus is alive, and Jesus saves. These are not only truths that we must be willing to defend—even die for—they are expressions of God's love toward us that should move us to love and care for everyone around us. In 1 Corinthians, the apostle Paul lays out the marks of genuine believers: faith, hope, and love. Note that these traits cause us to look outward, not inward; to be active, not passive; and to remain visible, not hidden. Our faith is anchored in the saving work of Christ in the past, and our hope enables us to look to the future as we wait for Christ's return. Love, however, is capable of disarming those who oppose us now as we serve and forgive them—a reflection of the grace and forgiveness God first extended to us.

THE DANGER OF COMPLACENCY

In June 1978, Russian dissident Aleksandr Solzhenitsyn—a devout Christian who had survived torture and deprivation in the Soviet gulags—gave the commencement address at Harvard University. In that address, he said, "There are meaningful warnings that history gives a threatened or perishing society. They are, for instance, the decadence of art, or a lack of great statesmen."[7]

I believe we are living in times that Solzhenitsyn foretold—times in which a lack of great statesmen serves as a warning that our civilization is threatened or already perishing. In the 2016 presidential election campaign, the election came down to a choice between two very flawed individuals, Donald Trump and Hillary Rodham Clinton. In pointing out that they were flawed candidates, I don't think I'm saying anything controversial—or anything the candidates themselves would deny. I'm not judging their hearts. I'm just stating the obvious.

We are all flawed human beings, and Christians are not perfect, only forgiven. But I'm not talking here about the kinds of flaws that are common to us all.

Both Mr. Trump and Mrs. Clinton seemed to carry an extraordinary amount of baggage. Mr. Trump, for instance, has made a number of poor moral choices. In his book *The Art of the Comeback*, Mr. Trump bragged of his adulterous affairs: "If I told the real stories of my experiences with women, often seemingly very happily married and important women, this book would be a guaranteed best-seller (which it will be anyway!)."[8] He made lewd comments in a taped conversation with celebrity reporter Billy Bush that were publicized just a month before the election. Mr. Trump was insulting and demeaning toward his critics and political opponents. He boasted about his wealth, his accomplishments, and his attractiveness to women. Litigation over fraud allegations related to Trump University continued throughout the campaign.

When I ponder the words of Aleksandr Solzhenitsyn, and I ask myself what a "great statesman" looks like, I think of someone who is temperate, self-controlled, respectable, above reproach, and not a lover of money or unfaithful to his wife—qualities that the apostle Paul lists as requirements for being an "overseer" or leader in the church (see 1 Timothy 3:2-12). Those are statesmanlike qualities, and by that standard, Mr. Trump does not qualify as such a leader.

(I am informed by a Christian friend who is close to the situation that, around the time Mr. Trump chose Mike Pence of Indiana as his running mate, he told close associates he was seeking to walk with God. It's worth noting that Vice President Pence is a committed, Bible-believing Christian, and at least eight other people President Trump appointed to top positions in his administration are known to be Christians. Though no one but God and Mr. Trump can truly know the state of his heart, I pray that he will earnestly seek God's will and God's wisdom.)

At the same time, our only alternative was former secretary of state Hillary Rodham Clinton. Throughout the campaign, Secretary Clinton was dogged by questions about her private e-mail server, on which she had kept classified State Department e-mails. According to then-FBI director James Comey, 110 e-mails on the Clinton private server contained information that was classified—confidential, secret, or top secret. Another 2,000 e-mails on the server contained sensitive information that the State Department later marked classified. Director Comey concluded that Mrs. Clinton had been "extremely careless" with our nation's secrets.[9]

The campaign was also hampered by suspicion of corruption involving Bill and Hillary Clinton's private charity, the Clinton Foundation. The *New York Post* reported:

> The Clinton family's mega-charity took in more than $140 million in grants and pledges in 2013 but spent just $9 million on direct aid.

The group spent the bulk of its windfall on administration, travel, and salaries and bonuses, with the fattest
payouts going to family friends.[10]

The Clinton Foundation raked in nearly $2 billion from 2001
to 2015, much of it from corporations, financiers, and foreign
governments, including Saudi Arabia, the United Arab Emirates,
and Oman.[11]

Given the many questions related to Clinton's activities both
during and after her time as secretary of state, we have to ask
ourselves, is this the track record of a "great statesman" (or in this
case, a "great stateswoman")? Is Mrs. Clinton someone who is
temperate, self-controlled, respectable, above reproach, not a lover
of money, and faithful?

You might ask why I am bringing all this up again. Weren't the
flaws and failings of Mr. Trump and Mrs. Clinton widely reported
by the news media in 2016? Of course they were. All of these facts
are well known to anyone who was following the campaign news.
My point is simply this: Aleksandr Solzhenitsyn seemed to be
speaking prophetically when he said that one sign of a "threatened
or perishing society" is "a lack of great statesmen."

I believe God was trying to get our attention in the fall of 2016.
This is just my opinion, and I don't claim to have biblical authority to back up this belief. But I wonder if God didn't allow us to
go through that difficult election season because He was calling
us to humble ourselves and pray and seek His face and turn from
our wicked ways.

I have talked to scores and scores of Christians who poured
out their hearts in prayer over that election. Everyone expected
that Mrs. Clinton would win the White House. As late as election

eve, the polls clearly indicated she was leading in key states. Many Christians were anguished that a candidate who had flouted the law in the e-mail scandal, who had demonstrated incompetence and dishonesty in the Benghazi disaster, and who supported unrestricted abortion on demand was going to be our next president.

But on election night 2016, Donald Trump was elected, and the nation was stunned. Some Christians considered his upset victory to be an answer to prayer—not because he was such a paragon of statesmanlike virtue. No, it was simply because many Christians believed that the alternative would lead us further down the road of decline and destruction.

Elections never catch God by surprise. He does not side with Republicans or Democrats, Libertarians or Greens. God can use any leader to accomplish His purpose. We know this, because in the Bible we have seen how he used even ungodly kings such as Nebuchadnezzar of Babylon and Cyrus of Persia to achieve His purpose.

I think the 2016 election was not so much about politics as it was about *prayer*. God wanted His people to *pray*. If we, as God's people, prayed fervently all year round for our nation and our leaders, we wouldn't face such difficult and troubling decisions on Election Day. God would raise up authentic statesmen and stateswomen to serve as our leaders. Many of God's people prayed for a miracle in the 2016 election and in the end voted for the candidate they saw as highly flawed but whose platform and campaign promises better represented their values and principles.

I also believe that our nation continues to be in grave danger, and the greatest danger we face is complacency. We Americans have a tendency, once an election is over, to simply go back to our old way of life, our careers, and our families, and then ignore what our leaders are doing in our name. This is no time for complacency. We need to watch our elected representatives closely. We need to hold them accountable for their actions. We need to watch how they vote, and we need to call and e-mail them frequently, urging them to act and vote according to godly principles and truths.

We must never forget that, as abolitionist Wendell Phillips once said, "Eternal vigilance is the price of liberty."

APPROACHING THE POINT OF NO RETURN

When we speak the truth to our post-truth world, we should expect opposition and persecution. We should expect to be treated no better than the prophets in Old Testament times. Before God sent Judah into exile in Babylon, He sent the prophet Jeremiah to remind the people that God had promised judgment if they fell away from Him. When Jeremiah delivered his message to the people, there was still time for them to turn to God for healing and forgiveness.

But the people of Judah didn't believe judgment was coming. They didn't believe God would keep His word. Perhaps they thought that God no longer punished disobedience as in times past. Perhaps they thought that God had evolved, that He had changed with the times. Perhaps they even thought, *God won't punish us. After all, we are His people. There is no need for repentance. Love wins!*

But the day eventually came when God's patience ended. The vast army of the Babylonians encircled Jerusalem and laid siege to the walls and gates. The people prayed for deliverance, but it was too late. They had passed the point of no return. Many were slaughtered, and the rest were led away in captivity. The city and its temple were laid waste.

For some reason, we in America think that our country is invincible. America will always be wealthy, powerful, and free. In spite of all the immorality, violence, rebelliousness, and sin in our nation, even many Christians think we're immune to God's judgment—just as the people of ancient Israel once thought.

Is God's judgment inevitable? No—there is still time to repent. How much time? I don't know. But I do know this: We can repent right now. Today. This very moment. And we *must*.

Are we listening to what God is saying to us through His Word? Are we listening to what He is saying to us through the political process? I hope and pray that we are.

Finally, I want to say something more about the title of this book. Who is our enemy? Why is this enemy described as "hidden"?

Is the hidden enemy ISIS or Al Qaeda?

Is the hidden enemy the Muslim religion?

Is the hidden enemy the atheists and secularists in our society?

Is the hidden enemy the political left? The political right?

Is the hidden enemy the religious left? The religious right?

The title of this book doesn't refer to any of these groups.

Well, is the hidden enemy Satan?

It's true that Satan is certainly our chief foe, our invisible enemy who attacks us and tempts us and opposes us from the invisible spiritual realm. The apostle Paul tells us that we are engaged in spiritual warfare, and Satan is a formidable enemy who controls the "evil rulers and authorities of the *unseen* world" (Ephesians 6:12, NLT, emphasis added).

But the title of this book doesn't refer to Satan, either.

Then who is the hidden enemy?

The hidden enemy is us.

We are our own worst enemy. *We* must decide to obey God.

We must choose to turn to Him, humble ourselves, pray, and turn from our wicked ways. *We* must make the daily decision to stand firmly for God and speak His truth. *We* must love sacrificially and continually, drawing from the unending grace we've received from the Lord. *We* are the ones who will determine if America comes under God's judgment—or if America is spared for the sake of our children and grandchildren.

The hidden enemy—the enemy we fail to recognize, the enemy we refuse to acknowledge—is *us*. The hidden enemy is the self-ishness and sin that lurks within *us*. The hidden enemy is the self-deception, rebelliousness, and hypocrisy we irrationally cling to. The hidden enemy is our eagerness to rationalize and justify ourselves instead of repenting and turning from our wicked ways.

Yes, the enemy is *us*.

But what a friend we have in Jesus!

Can America be saved? God is calling to us, reminding us of His promise to forgive our sin and heal our land. He is the Author of history, and He will have the last word.

So let us lift up Jesus in our lives. There is no salvation under any other name. Jesus is the Way, the Truth, and the Life. His truth is the only hope for a post-truth world.

ACTION AGENDA:
YOU CAN MAKE A DIFFERENCE

AS THE WEST MOVES FURTHER from its Judeo-Christian roots, can believers truly make a difference by refusing to remain in the shadows? Yes! In fact, the church's continuing influence is often most visible in the strongest storms.

When Hurricane Harvey lashed Texas and Louisiana in late August 2017, it was the first major hurricane to make landfall in the United States since 2005. Harvey was the wettest hurricane ever recorded in the continental United States, flooding thousands of homes. The storm killed eighty-three people—one in Guyana and eighty-two in the United States. Economic losses could top $100 billion; even more heartbreaking was the toll on individuals immediately after the storm.

"I lost everything," Adrian Rodriguez of Houston told a reporter as he surveyed the damage to his flooded home. The married father of three described some of his losses: "All my children's pictures of them growing up. Their birthday pictures. Vacation pictures. Their school projects of what they wanted to be when they grow up. . . . Everything in the house is history."[1]

Sixty-eight-year-old Chris Naylor of Bayside, Texas, had ridden out six other major tropical storms over the past several decades, but Harvey, with winds topping 160 miles an hour, was the worst. He said, "This is the first time I said to myself, 'If I get through this, then that will be the last one I ever ride out. . . . The wind was on all sides. Everything was flying." Naylor's home survived, but the plant nursery business he operated for twenty years is gone. He isn't sure he'll rebuild.[2]

In Refugio, Texas, a little church called Joy Ministries became God's outstretched hand of help to folks who had lost everything. "We were the only shelter in town," said Pastor Joel Garcia. "After the storm, people were just dropping people off." City officials lent a generator to the church to power the church's kitchen, which served four hundred meals daily to people who had lost their homes. Cook Manny Govella said, "I slept two hours a night. There was so much to do." Church members handed out supplies and helped people apply for aid.[3]

The federal emergency response agency, FEMA, was overwhelmed by the immensity of the disaster. Fortunately, nongovernmental organizations rushed in to help—the American Red Cross, the Salvation Army, and many others. But the most effective aid for people impacted by Harvey came from the church. Greg Forrester, head of the Voluntary Organizations Active in Disaster (VOAD), said, "About 80 percent of all recovery happens because of non-profits, and the majority of them are faith-based." Billions of dollars of relief funds, he said, are "raised by the individuals who go and serve, raised through corporate connections, raised through church connections."[4]

The Christian community's response to Harvey ranged from individual churches sheltering displaced people to large international organizations like Samaritan's Purse (the evangelical aid group founded by Franklin Graham) mobilizing truckloads of emergency supplies and cleanup equipment and sending them into the worst-hit areas.

In one instance, FEMA found itself playing more of a support role to Samaritan's Purse than the other way around. Just days after Harvey devastated parts of Texas and Louisiana, Hurricane Irma battered Florida. Most of Samaritan's Purse's disaster relief assets were already in Texas, so the organization had to bring equipment from Canada to Florida. A Samaritan's Purse official said that FEMA was "a big blessing to us, they're an assistance to us. . . . FEMA was instrumental in helping us clear that with customs and getting all the paperwork done."[5]

The Christian community's response to Hurricane Harvey was nothing new. Churches and parachurch organizations in the United States play a vital, preemptive role in disaster relief. Many groups stockpile bottled water, diapers, clothing, and other emergency supplies while training volunteer crews in everything from debris removal to helping people deal with government and private insurance bureaucracies. Why do Christians get involved with disaster relief? Why not let the government and the Red Cross handle the big crises?

Ed Stetzer, executive director of Wheaton College's Billy Graham Center and a senior fellow at its Humanitarian Disaster Institute, said that Christians respond "not out of a sense of guilt or a desire to impress but instead a longing to do unto others as, they believe, their God has done unto them. They see generous giving as a way to express their faith and live out Jesus' command to love God and neighbor above self."[6]

Hurricanes bring out the best in God's people—and there are many kinds of hurricanes in this world.

CULTURAL HURRICANES

When a scholar of the law asked Jesus, "Who is my neighbor?" the Lord replied with a story, the parable of the Good Samaritan (Luke 10:30-37). It tells us how we should respond in a crisis. In this story, a Jewish traveler is attacked by robbers, beaten, and left half-dead beside the road. Two deeply religious people, a priest and a Levite, notice the beaten man but pass by without stopping.

Finally, a Samaritan man comes by. The Samaritans and Jews are enemies. They despise each other. They have different religions, customs, and traditions, and they treat each other with contempt. But this Samaritan man doesn't see an enemy beside the road. He sees a *neighbor*. He bends down, treats the man's wounds, and takes him to an inn. The Samaritan even pays the innkeeper to care for the man.

The story tells us how we, as Christians, ought to respond to our neighbors who are victims of disasters, whether a robbery or a natural disaster like Hurricane Harvey. And who are our neighbors? They're not just people who live near us. They are people we have never met and probably never will meet in this life.

But that's not all. The story teaches us that our neighbors even include our enemies—the people we dislike; the people who hate us; the people who have a different religion or different customs and traditions from us. If we're going to take the teachings of Jesus seriously, we have to acknowledge that the secular leftist and the Islamist are also our neighbors.

These people may not value our culture, our principles, our faith, our way of life, or our freedom. In some cases, they want to destroy them. Yet they are our neighbors. We are to be Good Samaritans to them, even as we hold fast to the truth.

The crisis we face today is every bit as turbulent and deadly as the torrents of water and howling winds of the tropical hurricane. We are facing a *cultural* hurricane. We are facing a cyclone of ideas and ideologies that would seek to scour our faith off the face of the earth.

One of the most devastating cultural storms swirling through society today is the destructive idea of same-sex marriage. In chapter 4, I laid out the many ways freedom has come under attack since this practice was legalized in Great Britain in 2013, as well as my prediction that Americans will soon face similar restrictions following the Supreme Court's 2015 Obergefell v. Hodges decision.

By fall 2017, the debate over this issue was front and center in Australia as well. Despite the opposition raging against them there, many Christians refused to hide during this cultural storm. Just as the American Christians who reached out to help those devastated by Hurricanes Harvey and Irma model Christ-like mercy, these Australian believers can teach us much about how to respond with grace and truth during a societal storm.

AN AGENDA FOR ACTION

I was ordained to the ministry in the Sydney Anglican Diocese of Australia. I'm happy to say that this diocese has remained faithful to God's Word even as many Anglican churches elsewhere have drifted from orthodox positions.

The faithfulness of the Sydney Diocese is particularly important today as Australia goes through its own national debate on same-sex marriage. In September 2017, the Australian government mailed out survey forms containing a single question: "Should the law be changed to allow same-sex couples to marry?" While not binding, the results of the vote will be on the minds of the country's parliament before they vote on legislation to legalize same-sex marriage.

In Australia, as in the United States and Great Britain, same-sex marriage activists spout slogans of "tolerance" and "diversity" while threatening the lives and livelihood of anyone who disagrees with them. To his credit, Archbishop Glenn Davies of the Sydney Anglican Diocese has courageously spoken out on behalf of *real* tolerance and *real* diversity, which is the right to voice your pro-Christian, pro-traditional-marriage opinions without having to fear for your job, your life, or your family. In March 2017, he included the following in an opinion piece he wrote for the *Australian*:

> People . . . are starting to understand that the campaign for same-sex marriage is not sailing on a raft of rainbows but on a barge of bullies. . . .
>
> What kind of diversity is so monochrome that it does not allow differing expressions of opinion in the debate?
>
> Not only has this minority view tried to swamp the public debate with its introspective, authoritarian denial of free speech, it has struck at the heart of Australian democracy and the freedoms that we all cherish.[7]

As Davies points out, same-sex marriage activists go after traditional marriage supporters without mercy or conscience. This is no civilized debate over differing opinions. This is a blood sport, and the bullies of the secular left are determined to destroy their adversaries by depriving them of their careers.

Sydney pediatrician Dr. Pansy Lai appeared in a Coalition for Marriage advertisement in support of traditional marriage. In the ad, she said, "When same-sex marriage passes as law overseas, these kinds of programs become widespread and compulsory."[8] The programs she was talking about are designed to indoctrinate and teach schoolchildren that homosexuality is normal and are asked (for example) to role-play being in same-sex relationships.

Dr. Lai told reporters for the Australian Broadcasting Corporation that after her appearance in the advertisement, she and other staff members at the clinic where she works were threatened with violence. At the same time, a petition was posted on a website run by the left-wing activist group GetUp! claiming that Dr. Lai had "willfully spread misinformation and non-scientific evidence in order to promote the discrimination of LGBTIQ people in Australia" and called for her to be deregistered (stripped of her medical license).[9]

The petition quickly drew several thousand signatures, but also many complaints, and GetUp! removed the petition. A Coalition for Marriage spokeswoman responded, "In seeking to ruin the career of a doctor who dares disagree with its agenda, the same-sex marriage lobby has shown, yet again, that it has no interest in freedom of speech. The petition against Dr. Lai is a threat not only to her, but to any others who might try to voice their opinion. The message is loud and clear: agree on same-sex marriage or else."[10]

Many churches across Australia got involved in the national

conversation over same-sex marriage, including one near Sydney that convened a panel discussion designed to equip members to discuss this issue with friends, family, and coworkers. The speakers included a pastor from the church; the head of a Christian think tank that advocates for religious freedom in Australia; and a therapist who works with people who struggle with unwanted feelings of homosexual attraction.

The panel emphasized the importance of "speaking the truth in love" (Ephesians 4:15)—making a firm and uncompromised stand for the truth, yet doing so not out of anger or stubbornness or hate, but out of genuine Christian love for all people. The panel also encouraged members of the congregation to boldly share the gospel—not only with friends and neighbors but with opponents, like the ones who threaten the careers of people who believe marriage should be solely the union of one man and one woman.

This church emphasized truths we must all take hold of: We must speak the truth in love—even to those who reject the truth. We must speak the truth in love—even at the risk of our lives, our livelihood, and our reputations. We must speak the truth in love—because that is what it means to be a follower of Jesus.

When we speak the truth in love, we are serving our culture. Like the Good Samaritan, we are reaching out to our wounded enemy, an enemy who has been beaten and bloodied by sin, an enemy who does not want to be helped, an enemy who does not want our gospel or our Savior. It's risky business to offer aid to a wounded enemy. But that enemy is our neighbor, and Jesus calls us to serve our enemies, love our enemies, and be salt and light in a decaying and darkened culture.

God's design for families, for marriage, and for salvation leads to healing and hope for anyone who will receive it. Our gospel may fall on deaf ears. Our love may seem wasted on cold hearts. That's okay. God is responsible for the results—not us. Our only duty is to be faithful.

There is so much you and I can accomplish if we will follow the example of our Lord and proclaim His grace and truth. I'll close this book with a series of practical steps you can take to make a difference in your neighborhood, your church, your campus, and your world. Here is a three-stage Action Agenda to help you live faithfully for Christ in this post-Christian age:

Stage I: Learn the Truth

1. *Be a noble Berean student of God's Word.* As we saw on pages 97–98, the Bereans didn't take anyone's claims about Scripture at face value—and neither should we. Study the Word for yourself. Fact-check every claim you hear from a Bible teacher, TV preacher, or religious author. Some preachers and teachers are genuine messengers of God's truth—but some are false teachers. Don't rely on your own understanding. Instead, ask God to speak to you through His Word. Compare Scripture with Scripture. As Paul urged, be a student of the Bible who "correctly handles the word of truth" (2 Timothy 2:15). The search for God's truth is a noble quest.

2. *Read to examine and understand the foundations of your faith.* Commit yourself to a goal of reading one book per month. You can take books wherever you go (including the Bible in multiple translations) by installing a reading app on your phone. Whenever you have some downtime at the dentist's office or an airport, you'll always have a book with you. You don't have to spend a lot of money on a book-reading

habit. Use the library and read the classics for free via the Internet. Become informed on everything from Scripture to social trends, from the writings of Plato and Shakespeare to the great Christian writers like G. K. Chesterton, C. H. Spurgeon, C. S. Lewis, A. W. Tozer, and John R. W. Stott.

As you read, take time to study the foundations of your faith. Know why you believe. Know why you can trust the Bible as your standard of truth. Study the evidence for the Christian faith. Read authors like William Lane Craig, Norman Geisler, Gary Habermas, Hank Hanegraaff, John Lennox, Josh McDowell, Timothy McGrew, Lee Strobel, and Ravi Zacharias. As the apostle Peter wrote, "Always be prepared to give an answer to everyone who asks you to give the reason for the hope that you have. But do this with gentleness and respect" (1 Peter 3:15). Remember that your faith rests on a bedrock of verifiable truth.

3. *Be a skeptical—but active and involved—consumer of the news.* Learn to recognize bias and propaganda in the news stories you see and hear. Don't automatically believe news reports, but fact-check those reports and seek out sources that are reliable. Avoid consuming news only from outlets that merely confirm your biases. Fearlessly seek the truth, even if it means having to change your thinking. Don't be uninformed. Don't be misinformed. Be a smart and skeptical news consumer.

When you spot biased or dishonest reporting, take time to contact the news organization and ask for a correction or retraction. Write e-mails to the editor or ombudsman. Blog about stories that misrepresent the truth. Boldly, respectfully hold the news media accountable for accuracy and fairness.

Stage II: Stand for the Truth

1. *Practice absolute honesty and integrity.* Be truthful in your speech, your behavior, and your business dealings. Be trustworthy and dependable toward friends, coworkers, employers, and everyone else in your life. Build a reputation for absolute truthfulness so that you can speak God's truth with credibility and integrity.

2. *When talking to unbelievers or doubters, defend the truth with reason and evidence.* When you witness to unbelievers, they will sometimes reply, "All you have to go on is blind faith." Graciously, gently, but firmly refute that claim. Say something like "My faith isn't blind. Christianity is based on historical fact and reason. Our God is a rational God, and my faith is a rational faith." Then proceed to share the evidence for your faith. Don't feel as though you have to know it all. If a nonbeliever asks you a question and you don't know the answer, say, "That's a question I haven't thought about before. I'll look into it and get back to you." You can say this with confidence, knowing that the evidence you need will be there when you seek it.

   Defend God's truth in your church. You might be surprised at how many people in your congregation have adopted postmodern, post-truth attitudes toward God's Word. Get involved in a small group Bible study and get to know the issues that other church members are struggling with. Help them wrestle with doubts and questions from the perspective of God's Word. Help them to value the objective truth and proven principles of Scripture.

In your workplace or on your campus, become a defender of God's truth. If your coworker or professor makes false statements about the Bible or the historical Jesus or the Christian faith, challenge those statements—respectfully. If necessary, research the matter and come back prepared with the facts. Your goal is not to embarrass the other person or show how smart you are, but to speak God's truth. Start conversations with coworkers, neighbors, and fellow students and become a bold defender of the truth.

3. *Defend the First Amendment.* If a local university wants to shut down an event in order to appease protesters, get involved. Contact campus officials and urge them to have sufficient police protection to prevent violence and safeguard First Amendment freedom. Write letters to the local newspaper; contact the local TV news outlets; take your case to city officials, including the mayor and city council. Government officials swear an oath to protect and defend the Constitution, so hold them accountable for keeping that oath. Write blog posts, Facebook posts, Instagram posts, and tweets. Take a bold stand for the truth, and always be Christlike, courteous, and loving.

Stage III: Share the Truth

1. *Be a witness.* Commit to sharing the good news of Jesus Christ with the people around you—in your neighborhood, at work, and wherever you go. You don't have to preach. Just talk to people. Be friendly. Ask them where they go to

church, what they enjoy doing, what they care about most. Offer to pray for them. Show them you're genuinely interested in them, and be a good listener. If you are friendly and positive, you'll be amazed at how people open up and give you an opportunity to share your faith.

Jesus gave us two great instructions—the great commission and the great commandment. In the great commission, He said, "Go and make disciples of all nations, baptizing them in the name of the Father and of the Son and of the Holy Spirit, and teaching them to obey everything I have commanded you. And surely I am with you always, to the very end of the age" (Matthew 28:19-20). Are you carrying out the great commission in your daily life?

The other instruction Jesus gave us is the great commandment. Jesus said, "Hear, O Israel: The Lord our God, the Lord is one. Love the Lord your God with all your heart and with all your soul and with all your mind and with all your strength." Then Jesus added the second-greatest commandment: "'Love your neighbor as yourself.' There is no commandment greater than these" (Mark 12:29-31). If we truly love God with all our hearts, souls, minds, and strength, and if we love our neighbors as ourselves, we will naturally want to fulfill the great commission and spread the good news of Jesus Christ, making disciples wherever we go.

So let's pray for greater love, greater boldness, and greater eagerness to share the truth of the gospel with the people around us.

2. *Share the gospel with your Muslim neighbors.* There are more than four million Muslims in America. They are your

coworkers, your fellow students, your neighbors. Many American Muslims are willing to talk about their religion, and we can witness to them effectively if we show them genuine respect, Christian love, and friendship. Godly love makes evangelism possible.

Take time to read the Qur'an and become acquainted with its teachings. If the subject of Islamic terrorism comes up, tell your Muslim friend that you know that most Muslims don't support violence and that the terrorists don't represent what your friend believes. Establish a connection of trust. Tell your friend that you know the Qur'an presents Jesus as a miracle worker who even raised the dead. The Qur'an also presents Jesus as being born of a virgin and a man who lived a sinless life. Your friend will be pleased to know you are familiar with the teachings of the Qur'an.

Muslims have great respect for Jesus, whom they regard as a prophet. One of the great barriers to evangelizing Muslims is that they misunderstand the Christian doctrine that Jesus is the Son of God. They've been told that this means God had a sexual relationship with Mary. Of course, that's not what we believe. Avoid getting into an argument about what we *don't* believe; instead, focus on the truths we *do* believe.

The biggest difference between what the Qur'an teaches about Jesus and what the Bible teaches is that the Qur'an denies that Jesus died on the cross and rose from the dead. The Jesus of the Qur'an is a dead prophet; the Jesus of the Bible is a living and resurrected Savior.

Speak candidly about the essential features of the Christian faith: the Crucifixion, the blood of Christ, the death and burial of Christ, the Resurrection. Don't water down the story of Jesus to make it more palatable to your Muslim hearer. If your Muslim friend tells you the Bible has been corrupted (which is what Muslims are taught), you can say, without arguing, that you have always found the Bible to be in complete harmony with itself.

Use the great question evangelists have asked for years: "If you were to die today, do you know for certain that you would go to heaven?" Your friend will probably say no. This will give you an opportunity to share the hope within you. When your Muslim friend asks questions, answer as simply, directly, and briefly as possible.

Avoid using Christian jargon and metaphors. Speak in concrete terms about literal sin, the literal shed blood of Jesus, God's love and forgiveness that takes away our sin, and so forth. Quote biblical texts rather than merely giving your opinion. Be tactful, kind, respectful, and courteous.

Avoid criticizing Islam. Don't try to refute or debunk your friend's faith. Present your faith in a positive way, with clarity and sincerity. The gospel may irritate your friend, and that's okay. Just make sure it's the gospel that offends, not your behavior or attitude.

Before you talk to a Muslim, ask God for wisdom. Afterward, pray for God to reveal Himself to that person. If your friend becomes angry or defensive, back away for the moment—but keep the door open to future conversations.

Pray for your Muslim friend. God can change hearts through the power of prayer alone.

3. *Pray for your country and for your leaders.* Pray as an individual, pray as a family, and pray as a Bible study group or

church. God wants His people to humbly seek His forgiveness and healing power. "Blessed is the nation whose God is the LORD," the psalmist said (Psalm 33:12). And the apostle Paul wrote, "I urge, then, first of all, that petitions, prayers, intercession and thanksgiving be made for all people—for kings and all those in authority, that we may live peaceful and quiet lives in all godliness and holiness" (1 Timothy 2:1-2).

Let's pray for our government, our political leaders at every level, and the men and women in our military. Pray for judges and prosecutors and police officers. Pray for school board members and educators at every level, that they would stand for truth and that God would use them to influence lives in a godly way. Pray for the news media and entertainment media in America, that reporters and producers would be convicted of sin and would turn to God in repentance. Pray that the voters would seek God and His wisdom. Pray for spiritual revival and renewal throughout the land.

Pray that our leaders would be sensitive to the leading of the Holy Spirit. Pray that they would be convicted of their need for God and would recognize that they are accountable to Him for their decisions and actions. Pray that they would value and obey the Ten Commandments and the teachings of Christ. Pray that they would be honest and faithful in their duties. Pray that they would stand firmly against pressure, intimidation, and temptation. As the Scriptures tell us, "Righteousness exalts a nation, but sin condemns any people" (Proverbs 14:34).

Many people treat prayer as an exercise in passivity, a substitute for action: "Well, I guess there's nothing left to do but pray." But authentic prayer is active. It is the dynamic act of engaging with God and His promises to produce real change. And God always keeps His promises.

Remember that during the yearlong dictatorship of Mohamed Morsi in Egypt, Christians packed church services and all-night prayer meetings, defying the threats of Islamist gangs and thugs. There was never an hour of the day when Egyptian Christians were not calling upon God for justice and deliverance. As a result of that year of prayer, Egypt was delivered from its Islamist dictator and the downward course of the nation was reversed.

The same miracle can happen in America. The same miracle can happen in Great Britain. It can happen in France and Germany and anywhere Christians are willing to go to their knees in prayer for their nation. Do you love God enough to seek His mercy for your nation? Do you love your fellow human beings, your family, your children, and your grandchildren enough to pray for the nation they will live in, the nation they will inherit? Do you love your country enough to go to your knees, asking God to heal your land?

God is the Author and Finisher of history. "It is God who judges," said the psalmist. "He brings one down, he exalts another" (Psalm 75:7). This same all-powerful God has given us the amazing privilege of participating with Him in His eternal purpose through the power of prayer. We believe that prayer is not a last resort. It is the prime mover of people and events.

If we would change the world, then the place to begin is on our knees. Let's take action—meaningful action that will *literally* change the world. Let's pray.

THE EVANGELIST AND THE TERRORIST

HOW CAN YOU AND I HELP hold back the ideological hurricanes that are bearing down on our churches, our families, and our personal faith? In our own strength, it's impossible. But when we have turned our lives over to Christ and are empowered by His truth and grace, God can do much more than we could ever imagine.

Through Leading The Way's international ministry, I am privileged to hear incredible stories of transformation. The 24-7 satellite TV ministry of Leading The Way broadcasts the gospel across the Muslim world, from North Africa to Indonesia and the Philippines. We have a follow-up ministry on the ground in Muslim countries, so that those who watch these broadcasts and respond to the gospel can call, text, or e-mail and receive Christian counseling in their own language. Our follow-up coordinator is a man named Peter.

One day, Peter received a call on his cell phone, from the number we broadcast on our satellite channel. The call was from a man

I'll call Muhammad (not his real name). Muhammad said, "I need to meet with you."

One of the commonsense rules our follow-up counselors live by is: No in-person meetings until you know someone very well. Stay safe and make contact by phone.

But Peter felt the Lord telling him, *Go meet this man. I have plans for him.* So Peter obeyed this impulse from God and arranged to meet Muhammad face-to-face.

What Peter didn't know, and wouldn't learn until later, was that Muhammad was a "prince of ISIS," a leader of the terror organization that calls itself the Islamic State. He held such high rank that others in ISIS had sworn him allegiance. They would take orders from him and even die for him. He was also a high-ranking spiritual leader, a teacher of the Qur'an. He taught his followers to memorize the Qur'an, and he encouraged his followers to pursue jihad.

Peter later recalled his inner turmoil as he prepared to meet Muhammad, praying and meditating on God's Word. "I had a strange feeling that he was from ISIS," Peter said, "and that he might try to kill me. But I knew the Lord would protect me. God had a reason for this encounter, so even though I sensed danger, I was at peace."

Who was this prince of ISIS whom Peter was going to meet?

Muhammad later described himself in these words: "I grew up on radicalism. I was raised to take Islam back to the era of Muhammad, the era of power and conquests. I helped form groups to carry out jihad, to defend the country and Islam. One day, someone asked me why I am a Muslim. I had no answer. I began to search in the Qur'an, the Hadith, and the Sunnah. I wanted to find proof and evidence that Allah exists and Islam is right. I found nothing. I was troubled inside. I searched for answers.

I heard that this man Peter talked to Muslims about the Christian religion. I got his phone number and called him. When I went to my first meeting with Peter, I was afraid of what he might say to me. But I had to talk to him. I wanted the truth."

When the two men, the Christian evangelist and the Muslim terrorist, finally met, Peter looked the prince of ISIS in the eye and felt God speaking to him: *Be bold with him.*

Peter said, "Our God is not yours."

Muslims believe that Allah in the Qur'an is the same as the God of the Bible, but Peter had boldly, bluntly rejected that notion from the outset. Muhammad was filled with anger. Such arrogance! Peter's words had awakened the rage of the radical within Muhammad. "Because of my anger," he later recalled, "for a moment I forgot why I came to Peter. I had one thought: *How should I kill him?*"

Peter told Muhammad about Jesus, the one who had come to die as a sacrifice for our sins. Muhammad listened, but his thoughts were about murder. He had a knife in his boot. Killing this Christian would be easy.

Then without warning, Muhammad began to cry. Why? He didn't know. It wasn't anything Peter said. It wasn't anything Muhammad could identify. He just broke down—and because he was crying, he didn't go for the knife.

Peter recalled, "While Muhammad was crying, I put my hand on his shoulder and I prayed for him. As soon as I finished praying, he stood up and left me. I was relieved when he went away. I felt he was not stable. I felt that anything might happen."

Over the next few days, Peter prayed for Muhammad, asking God to work in this man's troubled heart. Finally Peter's phone rang again. Muhammad wanted another meeting.

At their next encounter, Peter saw that Muhammad seemed shaken and even more troubled than before. Muhammad said, "I had a dream."

"Tell me."

"You were in my dream. You came to me and gave me a white envelope dripping with blood. The blood had a sweet fragrance, like perfume. When I saw the blood, I was scared. Then you said to me, 'Don't be afraid'—and I awoke from the dream. What does it mean?"

"The blood in the dream," Peter said, "is the blood of Jesus that was shed for you. Without the shedding of blood, there is no forgiveness of sins."

"What should I do to be forgiven?"

"The Lord has given you His forgiveness—for free. You just need to accept it."

On that day, Peter began to disciple Muhammad. They met regularly to study the Bible and pray together. During one of their times together, Muhammad seemed burdened.

"What's wrong, Muhammad?" Peter asked.

"I have a confession. The first time I met with you, I had a knife and I intended to kill you. I'm sorry. I'm so sorry. In you, and in the Bible, I see a love that doesn't exist in Islam."

Muhammad grew quickly in his faith and in his hunger for the Bible. Soon he asked to be baptized. Today, the former prince of ISIS leads Bible studies for Middle Eastern Christians. He now says, "Jesus Christ is the truth. He is my life now."

Today, God is revealing His truth to many Muslims like Muhammad. If God can lead the prince of ISIS to the Prince of Peace, He can accomplish anything.

Is anything too hard for the Lord?

What does He want to accomplish through you?

NOTES

INTRODUCTION

1. Alan Feuer, "Linda Sansour Is a Brooklyn Homegirl in a Hijab," *New York Times*, August 7, 2015.
2. Bari Weiss, "When Progressives Embrace Hate," *New York Times*, August 1, 2017, https://www.nytimes.com/2017/08/01/opinion/womens-march-progressives-hate.html.

CHAPTER 1: THE TRUTH ABOUT OUR FUTURE

1. Dean R. Broyles, "A Gay-Marriage Pandora's Box?," *Los Angeles Times*, October 27, 2008, http://www.latimes.com/opinion/la-oew-broyles-jean27-2008oct27-story.html.
2. Arthur Delaney and Sam Stein, "Another Mass Shooting, Another Deluge of Tweeted Prayers," *Huffington Post*, December 2, 2015, http://www.huffingtonpost.com/entry/shootings-thoughts-prayers_us_565f57d5e4b08e945fedd2ad.
3. Gene Weingarten (@geneweingarten), Twitter, December 2, 2015, https://twitter.com/geneweingarten/status/672154567837118465?lang=en.
4. Becket Adams, "Reporters Scoff at 'Thoughts and Prayers' for Calif. Shooting Victims," *Washington Examiner*, December 3, 2015, http://www.washingtonexaminer.com/reporters-scoff-at-thoughts-and-prayers-for-calif-shooting-victims/article/2577517.
5. Jamie Dean, "Long Division: Activists at Both National Conventions Display the Challenges Donald Trump and Hillary Clinton Face," *World*, August 20, 2016, https://world.wng.org/2016/08/long_division.
6. Susan Olasky, "'Love,' Not Rights," *World*, August 20, 2016, 44.
7. Mark Tushnet, "Abandoning Defensive Crouch Liberal Constitutionalism," *Balkanization Blog*, May 6, 2016, https://balkin.blogspot.com/2016/05/abandoning-defensive-crouch-liberal.html.

8. Amy B. Wang, "'Post-Truth' Named 2016 Word of the Year by Oxford Dictionaries," *Washington Post*, November 16, 2016, https://www.washingtonpost.com/news/the-fix/wp/2016/11/16/post-truth-named-2016-word-of-the-year-by-oxford-dictionaries/.

9. Ted Koppel, "The Case against News We Can Choose," *Washington Post*, November 14, 2010, http://www.washingtonpost.com/wp-dyn/content/article/2010/11/12/AR2010111206508_pf.html.

10. Keith Olbermann, "Olbermann: False Promise of 'Objectivity' Proves 'Truth' Superior to 'Fact,'" NBCNews.com, November 15, 2010, http://www.nbcnews.com/id/40202512/ns/msnbc-countdown_with_keith_olbermann/t/olbermann-false-promise-objectivity-proves-truth-superior-fact/#.WbRSmciGOM8.

11. Ted Koppel, "Should Objectivity Still Be the Standard in News?" interview by Neal Conan, *Talk of the Nation*, NPR, November 16, 2010, http://www.npr.org/2010/11/16/131361367/should-objectivity-still-be-the-standard-in-news.

12. Michael Lind, "Western Civ Fights Back," *New York Times*, September 6, 1998, http://www.nytimes.com/1998/09/06/books/western-civ-fights-back.html.

13. Brian McLaren, *A Generous Orthodoxy* (Grand Rapids, MI: Zondervan, 2004), 35.

14. Brian McLaren, *A New Kind of Christianity: Ten Questions That Are Transforming the Faith* (New York: HarperCollins, 2010), 223.

15. Sue Reid, "As Islamic Extremists Declare Britain's First Sharia Law Zone, the Worrying Social and Moral Implications," *Daily Mail*, July 29, 2011, http://www.dailymail.co.uk/news/article-2020382/You-entering-Sharia-law-Britain-As-Islamic-extremists-declare-Sharia-law-zone-London-suburb-worrying-social-moral-implications.html.

16. Divya Talwar, "Growing Use of Sharia by UK Muslims," BBC, January 16, 2012, http://www.bbc.com/news/uk-16522447.

17. Michael Prell, *Underdogma: How America's Enemies Use Our Love for the Underdog to Trash American Power* (Dallas: BenBella Books, 2011), 13.

18. Ibid., 8.

19. Ibid., 13–14.

20. Francis A. Schaeffer, *A Christian View of the Church* (Wheaton, IL: Crossway, 1982), 401, emphasis in the original.

21. Nafeez Ahmed, "Pentagon Preparing for Mass Civil Breakdown," *The Guardian*, June 12, 2014, https://www.theguardian.com/environment/earth-insight/2014/jun/12/pentagon-mass-civil-breakdown.

22. Amanda Taub, "The Rise of American Authoritarianism," *Vox*, March 1, 2016, https://www.vox.com/2016/3/1/11127424/trump-authoritarianism.

CHAPTER 2: THE TRUTH BE HANGED

1. Heather Mac Donald, "Get Up, Stand Up," *City Journal*, April 9, 2017, https://www.city-journal.org/html/get-up-stand-up-15109.html; Matthew Ludlam and Matthew Reade, "Protestors Shut Down BLM Critic, Threaten Student Journalists," *Claremont Independent*, April 6, 2017.

2. Howard Blume, "Claremont College Suspends Students Who Blocked Access to Event with Pro-Police Speaker," *Los Angeles Times*, July 22, 2017, http://www.latimes.com/local/lanow/la-me-edu-claremont-students-suspended-20170722-story.html.

3. Matthew Reade, "Students Demand Administrators 'Take Action' against Conservative Journalists," *Claremont Independent*, April 17, 2017, http://claremontindependent.com/students-demand-administrators-take-action-against-conservative-journalists/.

4. Katherine Timpf, "Pomona Students: 'Truth . . . Is a Myth and White Supremacy," *National Review*, April 18, 2017, http://www.nationalreview.com/article/446862/pomona-students-truth-myth-and-white-supremacy.

5. Robby Soave, "Pomona College Students Say There's No Such Thing as Truth, 'Truth' Is a Tool of White Supremacy," *Hit & Run* (blog), Reason.com, April 17, 2017, http://reason.com/blog/2017/04/17/pomona-college-students-say-theres-no-su.

6. Charlotte Allen, "What on Earth Is Going On at the Claremont Colleges?" *Weekly Standard*, April 20, 2017, http://www.weeklystandard.com/what-on-earth-is-going-on-at-the-claremont-colleges/article/2007700.

7. Stephen Jay Gould, "Non-Overlapping Magisteria" in *Leonardo's Mountain of Clams and the Diet of Worms* (New York: Harmony Books, 1998), 269–284.

8. Richard Corliss, "Cinema: Our Critic Rides a Time Machine," *Time*, February 10, 1997, http://content.time.com/time/magazine/article/0,9171,985897,00.html.

9. Evelyn Beatrice Hall (under the name S. G. Tallentyre), *The Friends of Voltaire* (New York: G.P. Putnam's Sons, 1907), 199.

10. Associated Press, "Berkeley Police Criticized for 'Hands-Off' Approach to Violent Demonstrators," CBS Sacramento, February 7, 2017, http://sacramento.cbslocal.com/2017/02/07/berkeley-police-criticized-for-hands-off-approach-to-violent-demonstrators/.

11. Madison Park and Kyung Lah, "Berkeley Protests of Yiannopoulos Caused $100,000 in Damage," CNN.com, February 2, 2017, http://www.cnn.com/2017/02/01/us/milo-yiannopoulos-berkeley/index.html.

12. Natalie Orenstein and Emilie Raguso, "Eric Clanton Charged with Four Counts of Assault with Deadly Weapon," *Berkeleyside*, May 26, 2017, http://www.berkeleyside.com/2017/05/26/eric-clanton-charged-four-counts-assault-deadly-weapon/.

13. Charlotte Allen, "The Whole World Was Watching: The Appalling Protests at Evergreen State College," *Weekly Standard*, June 19, 2017, http://www.weeklystandard.com/article/2008391.

14. Lisa Pemberton, "80 Evergreen Protesters Sanctioned for Breaking Student-Conduct Code," *The Olympian*, October 1, 2017, https://www.seattletimes.com/seattle-news/80-evergreen-protesters-sanctioned-for-breaking-student-conduct-code/.

15. Peter Beinart, "A Violent Attack on Free Speech at Middlebury," *The Atlantic*, March 6, 2017, https://www.theatlantic.com/politics/archive/2017/03/middlebury-free-speech-violence/518667/.

16. Scott Jaschik, "The Aftermath at Middlebury," *Inside Higher Ed*, March 6, 2017, https://www.insidehighered.com/news/2017/03/06/middlebury-engages-soul-searching-after-speech-shouted-down-and-professor-attacked.

17. Kimberley Strassel, "The Left's War on Free Speech," *Imprimis* 46, no. 4 (April 2017), https://imprimis.hillsdale.edu/lefts-war-free-speech/.

CHAPTER 3: WHAT AMERICA IS—AND ISN'T

1. Douglas Brinkley, "How Tom Hanks Became America's Historian in Chief," *Time*, March 6, 2010.

2. David Horowitz, "The Biggest Racial Lie," *FrontPage Magazine*, May 26, 2016, http://www.frontpagemag.com/fpm/262978/biggest-racial-lie-david-horowitz.

3. Free the Slaves, "Trafficking and Slavery Fact Sheet, 2015," https://www.freetheslaves.net/wp-content/uploads/2015/01/FTS_factsheet-Nov17.21.pdf.

4. Kyle Becker, "Top 25 Most Racist Nations in the World: Where the United States Ranks Is Eye-Opening," *Independent Journal Review*, January 2017, http://ijr.com/2017/01/774469-top-25-most-racist-nations-in-the-world-where-the-united-states-ranks-is-eye-opening/.

5. William Carlos Martyn, *Wendell Phillips: The Agitator* (New York: Funk & Wagnalls, 1890), 185.

6. Thomas Jefferson, "Query XVIII: Manners," in *Notes on the State of Virginia*, TeachingAmericanHistory.org, http://teachingamericanhistory.org/library/document/notes-on-the-state-of-virginia-query-xviii-manners/.

7. Annette Gordon-Reed, *The Hemingses of Monticello: An American Family* (New York: W.W. Norton & Co., 2008), 99-100; Jon Meacham, *Thomas Jefferson: The Art of Power* (New York: Random House, 2012), 49.

8. Andrew Burstein, interview by Ken Burns, PBS.org, http://www.pbs.org/jefferson/archives/interviews/Burstein.htm.

9. US Congress, "Reports of Committees of the House of Representatives Made during the First Session of the Thirty-Third Congress" (Washington: A. O. P. Nicholson, 1854), 2:8–9.

10. Steven Morris, "The Founding Fathers Were Not Christians," Freedom from Religion Foundation, https://ffrf.org/publications/freethought-today/item/16866-the-founding-fathers-were-not-christians.

11. Daniel Webster, *The Speeches and Orations of Daniel Webster* (Boston: Little, Brown, and Co., 1914), 49.

12. Ibid., 525.

13. Kees de Mooy, ed., *The Wisdom of John Adams* (New York: Citadel Press, 2003), 35.

14. Ibid., 107.

15. George Washington, "General Orders, 2 May 1778," Founders Online, https://founders.archives.gov/documents/Washington/03-15-02-0016.

16. George Washington, "Address to the Delaware Nation, 12 May 1779," Founders Online, https://founders.archives.gov/documents/Washington/03-20-02-0388.

CHAPTER 4: SECULARISM: THE ENEMY WITHIN

1. Sam Harris, "What Is Secular Fundamentalism?," Big Think, video, 4:49 (transcribed by the author), http://bigthink.com/videos/what-is-secular -fundamentalism.

2. Maurice Caldeira, "Secular-Fundamentalism," top definition, Urban Dictionary, posted May 27, 2012, http://www.urbandictionary.com/define.php?term=Secular -Fundamentalism&utm_source=search-action.

3. Sam Harris, *The End of Faith* (New York: W. W. Norton & Co., 2005), 52–53.

4. Todd Starnes, "Starnes Exclusive: Chaplain Ordered to Remove Religious Essay from Military Website," *Fox News*, July 24, 2013, http://nation.foxnews .com/2013/07/24/starnes-exclusive-chaplain-ordered-remove-religious-essay -military-website.

5. Matthew Clark, "Victory: 'No Atheists in Foxholes' Article Reinstated on Chaplain's Website," American Center for Law and Justice, August 16, 2013, https://aclj.org /victory-no-atheists-in-foxholes-article-reinstated-chaplain-website.

6. Todd Starnes, "Student Claims Community College Rejected Application Because of Christian Faith," Fox News, April 24, 2014, http://www.foxnews .com/opinion/2014/04/24/student-claims-community-college-rejected -application-because-christian-faith.html.

7. Nicholas Humphrey, "What Shall We Tell the Children?" (Amnesty Lecture, Oxford, February 21, 1997), http://www.edge.org/3rd_culture/humphrey /amnesty.html; excerpted in a slightly different form by Richard Dawkins, *The God Delusion* (New York: Houghton Mifflin, 2006), 326.

8. Pablo Jáuregui, "Peter Higgs: 'No soy creyente, pero la ciencia y la religión pueden ser compatibles,'" *El Mundo*, March 1, 2013, translated from Spanish, http:// www.elmundo.es/elmundo/2012/12/27/ciencia/1356611441.html.

9. David Sergeant, "What's Changed in Britain since Same-Sex Marriage?" *Spectator Australia*, September 7, 2017, https://www.spectator.com.au/2017/09/whats- changed-in-britain-since-same-sex-marriage/; Sian Griffiths and Julie Henry, "Don't Man Up: Students May Lose Marks for Using 'He,'" *The Times*, April 2, 2017, https://www.thetimes.co.uk/edition/news/dont-man-up-students-may-lose -marks-for-using-he-t356wkdrq.

10. Laura Hughes, "Church Should Allow Same Sex Marriages and 'Keep Up' with Modern World, Justine Greenberg Says," *Telegraph*, July 23, 2017, http://www .telegraph.co.uk/news/2017/07/23/church-shoudl-allow-sex-marriages-keep -modern-world-justine/.

11. Sergeant, "What's Changed in Britain since Same-Sex Marriage?"

12. Adam Bienkov, "Liberal Democrat Leader Tim Farron Resigns in Order to Remain 'Faithful to Christ,'" *Business Insider*, June 14, 2017, http://www.businessinsider .com/breaking-liberal-democrat-leader-tim-farron-has-resigned-2017-6.

13. Rachael Pells, "Private Jewish School Fails Third Ofsted Inspection for not Teaching LGBT Issues," *Independent*, June 26, 2017, http://www.independent.co.uk/news /education/education-news/private-jewish-school-lgbt-issues-fail-ofsted-inspection -vishnitz-girls-london-orthodox-sex-british-a7809221.html.

14. Stephen Bates, "Anti-Gay Christian Couple Lose Foster Care Case," *Guardian*, February 28, 2011, https://www.theguardian.com/society/2011/feb/28/christian -couple-lose-care-case.

15. Henry McDonald, " 'Gay Cake' Row: Born-Again Christian Bakers Lose Court Appeal," *Guardian*, October 24, 2016, https://www.theguardian.com/uk-news /2016/oct/24/born-again-christian-ashers-bakery-lose-court-appeal-in-gay -cake-row.

16. Steve Bird, "National Trust Facing Membership Boycott over Gay Campaign," *Telegraph*, August 4, 2017, http://www.telegraph.co.uk/news/2017/08/04 /national-trust-facing-membership-boycott-gay-campaign/.

17. C. S. Lewis, *God in the Dock: Essays on Theology and Ethics* (Grand Rapids, MI: Eerdmans, 1970), 324.

18. Tobias Jones, "Secular Fundamentalists Are the New Totalitarians," *The Guardian*, January 5, 2007, https://www.theguardian.com/commentisfree/2007/jan/06 /comment.religion1.

19. Ibid.

CHAPTER 5: FINDING THE TRUTH IN A POST-TRUTH WORLD

1. Marc Ambinder, "'Brotherhood' Invited to Obama Speech by U.S.," *Atlantic*, June 3, 2009, https://www.theatlantic.com/politics/archive/2009/06/-brotherhood -invited-to-obama-speech-by-us/18693/.

2. Dr. Michael Youssef, interview by Don Lemon, *CNN Newsroom*, CNN, January 29, 2011, https://www.cnn.com/TRANSCRIPTS/1101/29/cnr.08.html. Some quotes have been lightly edited for readability.

3. Ryan Jones, "Why Did Obama Legitimize Terrorist Rule of Egypt?," *Israel Today*, February 3, 2011, http://www.israeltoday.co.il/NewsItem/tabid/178/nid/22643 /Default.aspx.

4. Andrew Gilligan and Alex Spillius, "Barack Obama Adviser Says Sharia Law Is Misunderstood," *Telegraph*, October 8, 2009, http://www.telegraph.co.uk /news/worldnews/barackobama/6274387/Obama-adviser-says-Sharia-Law-is -misunderstood.html.

5. Discover the Networks, "Mohamed Elibiary," DiscoverTheNetworks.org, http:// www.discoverthenetworks.org/individualProfile.asp?indid=2560.

6. "Egyptian Armed Forces Give Morsi Ultimatum: Respond to Protests or Military Will," PBS, July 1, 2013, http://www.pbs.org/newshour/bb/world-july-dec13 -egypt1_07-01/.

7. https://obamawhitehouse.archives gov/the-press-office/2013/07/03/statement -president-barack-obama-egypt

8. Abigail Abrams, "Pizzagate Gunman: 'I Regret How I Handled' Comet Ping Pong Shooting," *Time*, December 8, 2016, http://time.com/4594988/pizzagate-g/.

9. Skye Jethani, "Farewell, Louie Giglio?" *CT Pastors*, January 2013, http://www.christianitytoday.com/pastors/2013/january-online-only/farewell-louie-giglio.html.

10. Denny Burk, "Did the White House Force Giglio Out?" January 11, 2013, *Denny Burk* (blog), http://www.dennyburk.com/did-the-white-house-force-giglio-out/.

11. John Nolte, "Memory Holed: New York Times Reported White House Forced Pastor to Quit Inauguration," *Breitbart*, January 14, 2013, http://www.breitbart.com/big-journalism/2013/01/14/nyts-reports-white-house-forced-pastor-out/.

12. Becky Bowers, "President Barack Obama's Shifting Stance on Gay Marriage," PolitiFact.com, May 11, 2012, http://www.politifact.com/truth-o-meter/statements/2012/may/11/barack-obama/president-barack-obamas-shift-gay-marriage/.

13. Randy Alcorn, *Truth: A Bigger View of God's Word* (Eugene, OR: Harvest House, 2017), 211–12.

CHAPTER 6: WILL POLITICAL ISLAM DESTROY WESTERN CIVILIZATION?

1. Kate Samuelson, "Read Prime Minister Theresa May's Full Speech on the London Bridge Attack," June 4, 2017, *Time*, http://time.com/4804640/london-attack-theresa-may-speech-transcript-full/.

2. Hope Hodge Seck, "SpecOps Commander: 60,000 ISIS Fighters Killed by US Troops," Military.com, February 14, 2017, http://www.military.com/daily-news/2017/02/14/specops-commander-60000-isis-fighters-killed-by-us-troops.html.

3. Glen Carey, "Al-Qaeda in Yemen Seen Stronger Than Ever as War Wears On," *Bloomberg Politics*, February 2, 2017, https://www.bloomberg.com/politics/articles/2017-02-02/al-qaeda-in-yemen-seen-stronger-than-ever-as-war-wears-on.

4. "Bin Laden's Son Wants to Avenge His Father, Ex-FBI Agent Says," CBS News, May 12, 2017, http://www.cbsnews.com/news/preview-the-bin-laden-documents/.

5. Colin P. Clarke, "Al Nusra Is Stronger Than Ever," *The Rand Blog*, November 2, 2016, http://www.rand.org/blog/2016/11/al-nusra-is-stronger-than-ever.html.

6. Associated Press, "From Egypt's Leader, an Ambitious Call for Reform in Islam," *YNet News*, August 1, 2015, http://www.ynetnews.com/articles/0,7340,L-4612771,00.html.

7. Abraham Lincoln, "Lyceum Address," January 27, 1838, from *Collected Works of Abraham Lincoln*, ed. by Roy P. Basler et al., http://www.abrahamlincolnonline.org/lincoln/speeches/lyceum.htm.

8. Conrad Hackett, "5 Facts about the Muslim Population in Europe," Pew Research Center, July 19, 2016, http://www.pewresearch.org/fact-tank/2016/07/19/5-facts-about-the-muslim-population-in-europe/.

9. Richard Kerbaj, "Muslim Population 'Rising 10 Times Faster Than Rest of Society,'" *Times*, January 30, 2009, https://www.thetimes.co.uk/article/muslim-population-rising-10-times-faster-than-rest-of-society-2tr5r8kjzks.

10. Hugh Miles, "Two Faces of One of Islam's Most Important Clerics," *Telegraph*, July 20, 2005, http://www.telegraph.co.uk/news/uknews/1494397/Two-faces-of -one-of-Islams-most-important-clerics.html.

11. Mark Steyn, *America Alone: The End of the World as We Know It* (Washington, DC: Regnery, 2006), 146.

12. Alexandre del Valle, "The Danger of the Istanbul Process," August 8, 2012, *Alexandre del Valle* (blog), https://www.alexandredelvalle.com/single-post/2012 /08/09/The-Danger-of-the-Istanbul-Process.

13. Alexandre del Valle, "The Danger of the Istanbul Process," Gates of Vienna, August 8, 2012, https://gatesofvienna.net/2012/08/the-danger-of-the-istanbul-process/.

14. Clare M. Lopez, "Free Speech Champions Fight Back against OSCE 'Islamophobia' Industry," Center for Security Policy, October 11, 2016, https://www.centerfor securitypolicy.org/2016/10/11/free-speech-champions-fight-back-against-osce -islamophobia-industry/.

CHAPTER 7: ILLUSION AND DELUSION—OR TRUTH?

1. Lynn Barber, "I Took an Asylum Seeker into My Home. It Didn't End Well," *Sunday Times*, May 28, 2017, https://www.thetimes.co.uk/article/lynn-barber-i -took-an-asylum-seeker-into-my-home-it-didn-t-end-well-xtzn7gw99.

2. "Asylum Statistics," Eurostat, last modified June 21, 2017, http://ec.europa.eu /eurostat/statistics-explained/index.php/Asylum_statistics.

3. Ruth Sherlock and Colin Freeman, "Islamic State 'Planning to Use Libya as Gateway to Europe,'" *Telegraph*, February 17, 2015, http://www.telegraph.co.uk /news/worldnews/islamic-state/11418966/Islamic-State-planning-to-use-Libya-as -gateway-to-Europe.html.

4. Amber Athey, "BBC Anchor: We Have 'to Get Used to' Terror Attacks [Video]," *Daily Caller*, May 23, 2017, video transcribed by the author, http://dailycaller .com/2017/05/23/bbc-anchor-we-have-to-get-used-to-terror-video/.

5. Shane Ferro, "How Economic Inequality Makes Terror Attacks More Likely," *Huffington Post*, December 1, 2015, http://www.huffingtonpost.com/entry /thomas-piketty-terrorism_us_565e24d2e4b08e945fed3e38.

6. Susan Jones, "State Dep't: 'We Cannot Kill Our Way Out of This War,'" *CNS News*, February 17, 2015, http://www.cnsnews.com/news/article/susan-jones/state-dept-we -cannot-kill-our-way-out-war.

7. Paul K. Davis and Kim Cragin, eds., "Social Science for Counterterrorism: Putting the Pieces Together," RAND Corporation (2009), xxiv, https://www.rand.org/ content/dam/rand/pubs/monographs/2009/RAND_MG849.pdf; Alan B. Krueger and Jitka Maleckova, "Education, Poverty, Political Violence and Terrorism: Is There a Causal Connection?" Working Paper 9074, National Bureau of Economic Research (July 2002), 5, http://www.nber.org/papers/w9074.pdf?new_window=1.

8. Giulio Meotti, "Islamic Terrorists Not Poor and Illiterate, but Rich and Educated," Gatestone Institute International Policy Council, November 19, 2016, https://www .gatestoneinstitute.org/9343/terrorism-poverty-despair.

9. Dave Urbanski, "Two-Thirds of British Muslims Said in 2016 Poll They Wouldn't Share Terrorist Info with Police," *Blaze*, May 24, 2017, http://www.theblaze.com /news/2017/05/24/two-thirds-of-british-muslims-said-in-2016-poll-they-wouldnt -share-terrorist-info-with-police/.

10. Qur'an 8:12, Muhammad Habib Shakir, trans., in *Three Translations of the Koran (Al-Qur'an) Side by Side*, trans., Abdullah Yusuf Ali, Marmaduke Pickthall, and Mohammad Habib Shakir, http://www.gutenberg.org/files/16955/16955.txt.

11. Office of Senator Dianne Feinstein, "Feinstein Speaks at Supreme Court Nomination Hearing," press release, March 20, 2017, https://www.feinstein .senate.gov/public/index.cfm/press-releases?id=745D797F-76F1-4EB0-8ACD -388BDA95A4D8.

12. Brian Ross and Rehab El-Buri, "Obama's Pastor: God Damn America, U.S. to Blame for 9/11," ABC News, March 13, 2008, http://abcnews.go.com/Blotter /DemocraticDebate/story?id=4443788&page=1.

13. Cathleen Falsani, "Obama on Faith: The Exclusive God Factor Interview," CathleenFalsani.com, http://www.cathleenfalsani.com/?page_id=3146.

14. Becky Bowers, "President Barack Obama's Shifting Stance on Gay Marriage," Politifact.com, May 11, 2012, http://www.politifact.com/truth-o-meter /statements/2012/may/11/barack-obama/president-barack-obamas-shift -gay-marriage/.

15. Philip Francis and Mark Longhurst, "How LGBT Students Are Changing Christian Colleges," *Atlantic*, July 23, 2014, https://www.theatlantic.com /education/archive/2014/07/gordon-college-the-new-frontier-of-gay-rights /374861/.

16. "About," Young Pioneer Tours, http://www.youngpioneertours.com/.

17. Gopal Ratnam, "White House Unveils Call for 'Strategic Patience,'" *Foreign Policy*, February 5, 2015, http://foreignpolicy.com/2015/02/05/white-house-to -unveil-call-for-strategic-patience-russia-ukraine-syria-iraq-china-asia/.

18. Fox News, "Otto Warmbier's Parents Open Up about Son's Torture by North Korea: 'They are Terrorists,'" FoxNews.com, September 26, 2017, http://www .foxnews.com/us/2017/09/26/otto-warmbiers-parents-open-up-about-sons -torture-by-north-korea-are-terrorists.html.

19. Cheryl Vari, "Otto Warmbier's Parents: N. Korea 'Destroyed Him,'" Cincinnati .com, September 26, 2017, http://www.cincinnati.com/story/news/2017/09/26 /otto-warmbiers-parents-they-destroyed-him/703070001/.

20. Paul LeBlanc, "Who Was Otto Warmbier?," CNN, June 19, 2017, http://www .cnn.com/2017/06/16/us/otto-warmbier-profile/index.html; Merrit Kennedy, "Family Says Otto Warmbier, American Released by North Korea, Has Died," NPR, June 19, 2017, http://www.npr.org/sections/thetwo-way/2017/06/19 /533561000/family-says-otto-warmbier-american-released-by-north-korea-has-died.

21. David Choi, "John McCain: Otto Warmbier Was 'Murdered by the Kim Jong-Un Regime,'" *Business Insider*, June 19, 2017, http://www.businessinsider.com/otto -warmbier-murdered-by-north-korea-john-mccain-statement-2017-6.

CHAPTER 8: IS GOD'S JUDGMENT INEVITABLE?

1. Edward McNall Burns, *Western Civilizations: Their History and Their Culture* (New York: Norton, 1968), 237.
2. Jeremiah F. O'Sullivan, trans., *The Writings of Salvian, the Presbyter* (Washington, DC: The Catholic University of America Press, 1947), 193–194, 222.
3. David M. Walker, *Comeback America: Turning the Country Around and Restoring Fiscal Responsibility* (New York: Random House, 2009), 36–37.
4. Niall Ferguson, "Complexity and Collapse: Empires on the Edge of Chaos," *Foreign Affairs* 89, no. 2, (March/April 2010), https://www.foreignaffairs.com /articles/united-states/2010-03-01/complexity-and-collapse.
5. Warren W. Wiersbe, *The Wiersbe Bible Commentary: Old Testament* (Colorado Springs: David C. Cook, 2007), 1310.
6. John Bingham, "Church of England Cannot Carry On as It Is Unless Decline 'Urgently' Reversed—Welby and Sentamu," *Telegraph*, January 12, 2015, http:// www.telegraph.co.uk/news/religion/11340590/Church-of-England-cannot-carry -on-as-it-is-unless-decline-urgently-reversed-Welby-and-Sentamu.html.
7. Aleksandr Solzhenitsyn, *Détente, Democracy, and Dictatorship*, 3rd ed. (New Brunswick NJ: Transaction Publishers, 2009), 87.
8. Donald J. Trump and Kate Bohner, *Trump: The Art of the Comeback* (New York: Times Books, 1997), 116.
9. FBI National Press Office, "Statement by FBI Director James B. Comey on the Investigation of Secretary Hillary Clinton's Use of a Personal E-Mail System," news release, July 5, 2016, https://www.fbi.gov/news/pressrel/press-releases /statement-by-fbi-director-james-b-comey-on-the-investigation-of-secretary -hillary-clinton2019s-use-of-a-personal-e-mail-system.
10. Isabel Vincent, "Charity Watchdog: Clinton Foundation a 'Slush Fund,'" *New York Post*, April 26, 2015, http://nypost.com/2015/04/26/charity-watchdog -clinton-foundation-a-slush-fund/.
11. Editorial Board, "Separate Philanthropy from Political Clout: Hillary Clinton Should Ban Foreign Donors to the Clinton Global Initiative," *New York Times*, February 20, 2015, https://www.nytimes.com/2015/02/20/opinion/hillary -clinton-should-ban-foreign-donors-to-the-clinton-global-initiative.html.

CHAPTER 9: ACTION AGENDA: YOU CAN MAKE A DIFFERENCE

1. Associated Press, "New Floods Possible in Houston as Thousands Return After Harvey," CBC News, September 3, 2017, http://www.cbc.ca/news/world/harvey -texas-return-home-1.4273775.
2. Jessica Priest, John Wilcox, and Marina Riker, "Day 5: 'At Least God Let Us Live,'" *Victoria Advocate*, August 28, 2017, https://www.victoriaadvocate.com/news/2017 /aug/28/at-least-god-let-us-live/.

3. Gabriella Canales, "Church Offers Refuge for Devastated Town," *Victoria Advocate*, September 4, 2017, https://www.victoriaadvocate.com/news/2017/sep/04/refugio -church-offers-shelter-supplies/.

4. Paul Singer, "Faith Groups Provide the Bulk of Disaster Recovery, in Coordination with FEMA," *USA Today*, September 10, 2017, https://www.usatoday.com/story /news/politics/2017/09/10/hurricane-irma-faith-groups-provide-bulk-disaster -recovery-coordination-fema/651007001/.

5. Ibid.

6. Ed Stetzer, "Remember Teachings of Mr. Rogers and the Good Samaritan in Harvey Relief Efforts," *USA Today*, August 31, 2017, https://www.usatoday.com /story/opinion/2017/08/31/harvey-relief-efforts-remember-teachings-mr-rogers -and-good-samaritan-ed-stetzer-column/615904001/.

7. Anglican Church League, "Anglican Archbishop Glenn Davies Slams Same-Sex Marriage Activists," *Anglican Church League*, March 31, 2017, http://acl.asn.au /anglican-archbishop-glenn-davies-slams-same-sex-marriage-activists/.

8. Lily Mayers and Ky Chow, "Same-Sex Marriage Survey: Petition to Deregister Pansy Lai, Doctor in No Campaign Ad, Taken Down," ABC News (Australia), September 4, 2017, http://www.abc.net.au/news/2017-09-04/same-sex-marriage -petition-against-doctor-pansy-lai-taken-down/8869260.

9. Nic White, "How's That for Equal Rights? Woman Doctor Who Appeared in 'No' Ad for Gay Marriage Vote Subjected to a Campaign to Have Her Stripped of Her Medical Licence," *Daily Mail*, September 3, 2017, http://www.dailymail.co.uk/news /article-4848708/Gay-marriage-activists-want-Dr-Pansy-Lai-deregistered.html.

10. Mayers and Chow, "Same-Sex Marriage Survey."

We are witnessing the book of Acts being lived out today in the Middle East. Thousands of Muslims are coming to faith in Jesus Christ.

After reading the miraculous story of Muhammad, the former prince of ISIS, you may be asking, "How can I be part of this move of the Holy Spirit in the Muslim world today?"

You can make it possible for untold numbers of Muslims like Muhammad to come to Christ by partnering with us at Leading The Way. Together with partners around the world, we are proclaiming the gospel through 24-7 broadcasting, discipling new believers in closed countries, and helping the persecuted—and God is doing the impossible. As Muhammad said, *"I spent thirty years of my life serving Satan. I was urging people toward jihad. But when I interacted with Leading The Way's follow-up team and heard the gospel, I experienced a love that doesn't exist within Islam. At first I was fearful of accepting the Christian faith . . . but I wanted the truth. And I found the truth in Jesus Christ."*

JOIN THE MOVEMENT TO PROCLAIM, DISCIPLE, AND HELP.

Learn more and partner with us today at LTW.org.

www.tyndalemomentum.com

CP1341